Blessings,

Doris Frame

Num 6:24-26

If you think *Blended and Blessed* is just for members of blended families, you need to think again. In this honest, practical, biblical book, Inés Franklin provides a set of beautiful principles from the Beatitudes that will benefit any member of any family—blended or not. Far from being a second-class picture of God's design for the family, the blended family Franklin envisions is "a powerful testimony of God's grace and ability to bring unity where division once existed." Come to think of it, isn't that an accurate picture of God's forever family?

—STAN JANTZ,
Global Ambassador of Come and See Foundation

For more than seven years, I have seen Inés and her husband, Jim, graciously and consistently live the message of *Blended and Blessed*. Her life gives a lot of weight to her teaching—to the words in this book. And the words are so helpful and insightful. You will walk away with a beautiful vision for a blended family, practical insight from the Beatitudes, and wise and encouraging counsel. I highly recommend this book to those who are in a blended family and those who pastor, counsel, or encourage blended families.

—ERIC GEIGER,
senior pastor, Mariners Church

You are either part of a blended family or you know several, with their unique makeup, struggles, and accomplishments. Being part of a blended family can be overwhelming and very, very complicated. Inés Franklin's book, as a member of a blended family, provides clarity, hope, and practical tools. It's based on principles from Jesus' Beatitudes, informed by research, and presented from her own vulnerable story. You'll be touched and encouraged by the lessons Inés has learned about establishing family peace and wholeness.

—JOHN TOWNSEND, PH.D.,
Psychologist, author of thirty-five books, selling 15 million copies,
including the *New York Times* bestselling *Boundaries* series.
Founder, Townsend Institute of Leadership and Counseling
at Concordia University Irvine, and the Townsend Leadership Program

Insightful, yet easy to read, this resource points blended family couples and practitioners in the direction of growth and health. Encouraging and inspiring, this book will inform your journey and root it in eternal wisdom that illuminates the stepfamily experience.

—RON DEAL,
blended family trainer, therapist, and author of *The Smart Stepfamily*
and *Building Love Together in Blended Families* (with Dr. Gary Chapman)

Inés has given us a gift in *Blended and Blessed*. This book is refreshingly vulnerable, transparent, honest, faith-filled, and practical. It is for real people living real lives in real families. By applying one of the most important teachings of Jesus to family dynamics and relationships, Inés shows us that redemption and flourishing are possible for every family.

—CHRISTINE CAINE,
Founder A21 and Propel Women

Rooted in the teachings of Jesus in the Beatitudes, Inés Franklin's personal experience shines through every chapter of *Blended and Blessed*. In a style that is rich with wisdom and hope, she faces head-on the pain and complexity of navigating roles, expectations, and the roadblocks to healing and trust in a blended family. This is not a survival plan; it is a vision for the kind of wholeness only possible when space is created for the transformational grace of God.

—DR. MICHAEL BEALS,
President of Vanguard University

Inés has thoughtfully crafted a book that is more like a heart song for blended families who wish to integrate their faith into their healing and bonding process. Inés offers her own personal insights, latest research, and practical tools that have the potential to truly transform a blended family's culture. Inés' application of the Beatitudes speaks to the humility, vulnerability, and patience required in learning to love new family members well. I can't recommend this book enough as it touched me personally with my own journey of blending a family, and I pray this book becomes a Bible study for blended families in the church across our nation and beyond.

—DR. JENNA FLOWERS,
licensed Marriage and Family Therapist, author, speaker

Solomon observed that "there is no end to the making of many books" (Ecclesiastes 12:12), and there are often far more books written on a topic than wisdom represented in their many pages. But this book is different. First, it is on a topic hardly considered in the evangelical world, although it touches so many lives in churches. Second, it offers a perspective aimed at helping rather than condemning, building rather than destroying. All of us have been impacted by the reality of blended families today. But not all of us receive biblical and helpful wisdom. In this book, Inés Franklin offers hope from the words of Jesus Christ, with honest reflection from her family's journey. Countless people will be helped by this book!

—ED STETZER,
Dean at Talbot School of Theology at Biola University

Most Christian books live somewhere on the "spectrum": on one extreme, they lean towards solid theology but are silent toward human reality; on the other distant end, they lean strongly toward application but miss the incorporation of solid, timeless biblical truth. Inés Franklin's book, *Blended and Blessed*, is a refreshing exception. Solidly grounded in scriptural substance, she manages to use the short but powerful opening strains of Jesus' Sermon on the Mount to inform the challenge of following the Author of Functionality in a fallen world of dysfunction.

Well-illustrated from her own life story and honestly presented as the proof of God's redemptive power, this book will bring insight and inspiration to people who are often stuck in a sense of hopelessness that comes from a darkening cultural backdrop. The great headline, "blessed are you," is a promise that Jesus is still validating when His path forward is chosen by people who are dependent on Him to bring health to themselves and to the relationships they represent!

—BOB & CHERI SHANK,
Founders, The Master's Program

In a time of desperately needed discipleship in the Church, Inés Franklin is a steady, dependable Bible teacher pointing us to the Word of God. Her passion for a resilient faith is timely and contagious.

—LISA WHITTLE,
author and Bible teacher

FOREWORD BY JIM BURNS

Blended & Blessed

Building Family Unity & Healing
Through the Beatitudes

Inés Franklin

Published in association with The Fedd Agency, Inc., a literary agency.

Fedd Books
P.O. Box 341973
Austin, TX 78734

www.thefeddagency.com

Hardback ISBN: 978-1-964508-52-8

Library of Congress Control Number: 2026900738
First Edition
Printed in the United States.

Cover Design by Christian Rafetto (www.humblebooksmedia.com)

To my dearest "Smoothie" family,

My great love for you is beyond measure and endures forever.

TABLE OF CONTENTS

FOREWORD

You have in your hands a really good book. Not only is it well written and compelling, but it's also incredibly hopeful. You no doubt picked up the book because, like Inés Franklin, you are living in a "blended family." And I'm sure you will agree with Inés that blending a family is no simple task. It can be daunting. She reminds us that often our expectations clash with reality, and that can be disorienting. A man and woman fall in love, and too often they expect that everyone else in the family will all get along, and life will finally be happily ever after. Not so. She calls her blend "The Franklin Smoothie Family." It's a good description of what can become, but she is first to say it isn't easy, and we have to acknowledge there will be some (many?) bumps in the road.

I found three story lines in this book: 1. Inés has her own story, and it is woven throughout this book. Talk about trading dysfunction and pain for hope and inspiration. 2. Inés is a wonderful Bible teacher. She uses the Beatitudes from the words of Jesus as well as other biblical principles to provide sound insight and instruction. This woman can preach! 3. There are practical takeaways on every page. If you have a blended family, you will receive practical help about your own journey and a healthy way to blend on every page.

Let's talk about Inés Franklin for a moment. You will get to know her well through these pages. Her story is one of hope and healing. Her authenticity shines through on every page. Inés is what I call a "transitional generation person." Her family background and some of her life choices place her squarely in the category of dysfunctional. The Bible clearly tells us that we inherit the sins of our family to the third and fourth generation. Along the way, Inés made a decision to *recover* and not *repeat* those generational sins. She would be the first to admit that she is not perfect and that recovery may be a lifelong process, but healing is possible. She helps us understand that if we don't heal, we will repeat. She will give you a peek into her own life, and quickly you will understand that "if she can overcome, I can overcome." You can also read more about her life journey in her book, *Uncharted: Navigating Your Unique Journey of Faith.*

In this book, you will also receive excellent, trusted Biblical instruction. The Beatitudes of Jesus are a part of the Sermon on the Mount, which is undoubtedly the most popular sermon ever spoken and ever written. The wisdom of Jesus in these Beatitudes has inspired and challenged people for over 2,000 years. Many scholars believe these Beatitudes and the entire sermon are some of the most important words ever spoken or written. I love how Dale Bruner describes this message of Jesus: "The Sermon on the Mount is, spiritually speaking, actually the sermon from the valley. It starts low. It starts with those who feel very unlike mountains!" In my work with families who are trying to blend, they often feel more like they are in a valley than on the mountaintop. But you will quickly see in this book that there is hope and healing for those willing to receive God's mercy. You can break the cycles of hurt and dysfunction. Even if you have shied away from the Bible in the past, as you read this book, you will see the great insight and understand the importance of the Word of God for your life and your family.

As I mentioned, the practical takeaways are on every page. There is also a section at the end of every chapter called "Practical Tools." Don't miss them. This book may be best used when couples read it together or when you gather a small group to read and discuss it. I know of one group of moms who started meeting three years ago to read a book about dealing with their adult children, and they are still meeting, supporting each other, praying, and having fun together. I can't think of anyone blending a family who won't do better in a group. Perhaps this book is the catalyst you need to join a group of like-minded people. Everyone needs to learn practical skills, like navigating co-parenting, stepparenting, changing family roles, and managing unmet expectations, as well as understanding that God is good with our messes. He can handle them and help us clean up some of the messes we create. You will get all this and more in this book.

As you can tell, I'm a fan of Inés Franklin. Her work and impact as a staff member at Mariners Church in Irvine, California, is remarkable. This is a book I will pass out and recommend to all people in the blended family category. So, get ready to be challenged and inspired to live a "smoothie" kind of life that can be meaningful and life-changing. Changing the trajectory of your family legacy begins with you.

Jim Burns, PhD.
Founder, HomeWord
Author of *Doing Life with Your Adult Children: Keep Your Mouth Shut and the Welcome Mat Out*

THE
BEATITUDES

Blessed are the poor in spirit,
for the kingdom of heaven is theirs.
Blessed are those who mourn,
for they will be comforted.
Blessed are the humble,
for they will inherit the earth.
Blessed are those who hunger and thirst for righteousness,
for they will be filled.
Blessed are the merciful,
for they will be shown mercy.
Blessed are the pure in heart,
for they will see God.
Blessed are the peacemakers,
for they will be called sons of God.
Blessed are those who are persecuted because of righteousness,
for the kingdom of heaven is theirs.

You are blessed when they insult you and persecute you and falsely say
every kind of evil against you because of me. Be glad and rejoice, because
your reward is great in heaven. For that is how they persecuted the
prophets who were before you.

—MATTHEW 5:3–12

THE
CALL

You are the salt of the earth. But if the salt should lose its taste, how can it be made salty? It's no longer good for anything but to be thrown out and trampled under people's feet.

You are the light of the world. A city situated on a hill cannot be hidden. No one lights a lamp and puts it under a basket, but rather on a lampstand, and it gives light for all who are in the house. In the same way, let your light shine before others, so that they may see your good works and give glory to your Father in heaven.

—MATTHEW 5:13–16

INTRODUCTION

THE JOY AND HEARTACHE OF BLENDING

At birth, we enter the world crying and are welcomed into a family. In fact, crying is a natural and expected response in most healthy deliveries. It is also natural and expected that the lifelong journey of family life, with its profound bonds and inevitable challenges, evokes tears of both joy and heartache. In God's design of the sacred institution of the family, Jesus is our ultimate source of identity, love, grace, support, and intimacy; the family is our earthly expression of it. For this reason, family is of great importance, engaging us at the deepest emotional levels.

My husband, Jim, and I have a family of five children, their spouses, and ten grandchildren. Because we have so many social categories (step, half, adopted) in our family, we affectionately call ourselves the "Franklin Smoothie Family." We, of course, know that blending a family isn't as simple as tossing different ingredients into a smoothie. Defiant to the modern expectation of instant gratification is the reality that blending a family requires time, intentionality, and a great deal of grace. After all, we're uniting tender human hearts and forging new relationships, not just mixing frozen fruits and veggies. In many ways, this mirrors the family of God, where diverse individuals are woven together in love.* Isn't every family, whether blended through stepchildren, adoption, or even in-laws joining through marriage, blending different people, personalities, and experiences to form one larger family?

When couples form a blended family, it's natural to hope for a fresh start and expect a few tears. Many begin with rose-colored glasses, believing that the addition of love and commitment to our families will smooth out every bump along the way. I certainly did. The shock that comes when expectations clash with reality can be disorienting. But the very fact that we're "blending" indicates a fundamental change has occurred, either precipitated by something broken (like past loss or fractured relationships) or something beautifully added (such as adoption, new unions, or extended family ties). This book is for you who, like us, have faced (or are about to face) the exhilarating yet daunting task of blending a family. Here, I offer a path toward healing, unity, and Christ-centered growth through biblical wisdom and practical tools.

The timeless Christian answer—the life of simply following Jesus—is still the answer for you. *Yes, even if you're in a blended family.* In this book, I aim to inspire and guide you and your family to reflect God's redemptive love amid your unique challenges.

As a pastor and a matriarch of a complex blended family, I share my perspective—cultivated through decades of experience—alongside insights from psychologists, theologians, and social scientists. Expect a blend of personal stories, profound biblical insights, and interactive tools to equip you for Holy Spirit-led transformation. We'll explore family dynamics, including parenting, co-parenting, stepparenting, discipleship, and building a family culture and legacy. Each chapter provides

---

* See Mark 3:35, John 1:12-13, Romans 8:14-17, Ephesians 2:19, and Galatians 3:26. These passages emphasize spiritual adoption, where faith transcends biological or social boundaries, creating a new family identity under God's parenthood.

Scripture-based tools, including self-reflection exercises, healing discussions, and prayer prompts. These versatile resources can be completed alone for personal growth, discussed with a spouse or peer for deeper connection, or used in small groups to foster community healing, perspective, and accountability.

Each chapter of this book is rooted in a section of Jesus' Sermon on the Mount. So, before we embark on this chapter-by-chapter journey through the Beatitudes and Jesus' call to flourish, let's lay a foundation with essential insights into God's design for family life, the challenges of complex family dynamics, and the liberating truth of grace.

A Biblical View of Family

Even though I have experienced divorce and have my own complicated family, the biblical and historical view of marriage as a covenanted, lifelong, monogamous relationship between a biological man and woman is the firm foundation from which I write this book. Marriage and family serve as profound metaphors for the gospel, meant to be sources of love and so much more that is good. God designed the family as the foundation of our social existence. As we study the Bible, it's hard to miss that God intends for family to reflect his relational nature, love, and grace. God is triune, existing eternally in three distinct persons (Father, Son, and Holy Spirit) united in essence and purpose (see Matthew 28:19) and modeling perfect community. In Genesis 2:18, God declares it is not good for man to be alone and creates Eve as a companion for Adam. In so doing, the Creator of the Universe established the family as a source of continual support. The Psalmist reinforces this when he declares children as a blessing from the Lord, a divine gift for identity and intimacy (Psalm 127:3–5). God describes himself as a loving Father who shapes and cares for his children (Isaiah 64:8) and likens his tender compassion and comfort to a mother's nurturing care (Isaiah 66:13).

This pattern of imagery continues in the New Testament, where the apostle Paul instructs parents and children to honor and nurture one another, fostering a supportive environment rooted in grace (Ephesians 6:1–4). Jesus affirmed the importance of family by honoring his mother (John 19:26–27), yet he also redefined and expanded it, declaring that those who do the will of God are God's true family, encompassing all believers in a spiritual kinship (Mark 3:34–35). In fact, through Jesus, the family of God includes Gentiles, as Paul explains in Ephesians 2:19. Believers of every nation, tribe, people, and language are no longer foreigners but members of God's household, forming the ultimate eternal "blended" family.* In Christ, our identity as children of God is secure, and relationships are grounded in the biblical principle of covenant modeled for us by Jesus.

However, the introduction of human sin, shame, and broken relationships in Genesis 3 started a cycle of family dysfunction that has affected the human experience in every subsequent family. Since then, all families experience pain, dysfunction, and sometimes estrangement. Whether your family is blended or not, it must contend with the fallen nature of humanity, complex dynamics, and evolving roles. Blended families, however, face extra layers of challenge. As Romans 8:22–23 describes, all creation groans for redemption—a redemption that only Jesus offers—and our families are part of that groaning creation.

---

* See Revelation 7:9–17.

Complex Families

In our contemporary society, family structures are increasingly diverse and complex. A large percentage of families are not made up of two parents and their children. Today's families include single parents with children on a full- or part-time basis; stepfamilies incorporating "his," "hers," and shared offspring, either full- or part-time; foster care households; unmarried couples cohabiting with kids; childless couples; extended multigenerational homes; and same-sex partnerships. When referring to "homes in which children from a previous marriage reside," the literature uses terms such as blended, binuclear, reconstituted, and stepfamilies.[1] For the purposes of this book, I am utilizing these terms interchangeably. When I speak about a "blended family," I am including any family where new members join outside the direct biological line—such as half-siblings, stepsiblings, foster children, adopted members, or even in-laws—families built on love, commitment, and shared life, not just blood. Even biological families experience this complexity as the moment a child gets married, the process of blending families begins.

Blended families are also increasingly common, with recent data indicating that 1,300 new stepfamilies are formed each day, more than 10 percent of children in the United States live in blended families,[2] and over 40 percent of adults have at least one step-relative.[3] These families navigate differing parenting styles, handle past hurts from loss or fractured relationships, and redefine family roles. Building trust becomes a daily endeavor. While they contribute richly to society and can be a blessing through redemption in Christ, these families might see themselves or be treated as "second-class."

Far from being second-class, our families are a beautiful blessing to society. I believe that we can also be a living epistle for a better understanding of the family rooted in God's grace. Whether you are or aren't part of such a household, here are three reasons why I believe reconstituted families are a powerful reflection of God's grace and why they deserve our support and understanding:

- **Diversity and Growth**: They teach us about diversity, patience, and understanding as they often develop into a larger extended family, including "bonus" parents, siblings, and grandparents. The different backgrounds and traditions within the family create opportunities for growth and deeper connections. This creates a broader support network for children, providing them with access to more mentors, caregivers, and love, which benefits society by fostering stronger, more well-rounded individuals.

- **Strength in Unity**: Coming together to merge households requires intentionality, which can lead to strong bonds. Siblings and stepparents develop skills in adjusting to new roles, expectations, and dynamics, which are essential traits in today's fast-changing world. These families teach children (and adults) resilience, emotional intelligence, and the ability to embrace change.

- **A Picture of Redemption**: Families formed through remarriage are a reminder that God creates new beauty from brokenness. The journey, while challenging, reflects God's power to restore and redeem. By nature, these families bring together people with different histories who must work through misunderstandings, conflicting traditions, and even past hurts. The process teaches profound lessons about forgiveness, empathy, and the power of grace—qualities that resonate and ripple out into the wider community.

A blended family's journey requires perseverance and resilience. Even in complexity, this legacy of sticking together conveys to children and society the beauty and endurance of sacrificial love in a powerful way.

The Fallacy of Normal

As if navigating our own history isn't hard enough, one of the temptations for a blended family is comparing ourselves to so-called "normal" families. Biologically connected individuals might seem to lack some of our struggles. But is there truly such a thing as a "normal" family?

Sometimes, society tries to define "the normal family" for us. This is reflected in art. Sculptures dedicated to the idea of family are displayed in cities worldwide. For example, we can find *The Family*, a stainless steel sculpture located in Ireland, and *The Normal Family*, a terracotta sculpture located, ironically, in Normal, Illinois. Both represent an imagined ideal family. Both have sparked the debate about what is truly "normal."

The truth is, there is no such thing as a perfect or "normal" family, blended or otherwise. We can certainly talk about what's healthy or unhealthy, and we can identify what's statistically average or rare. But no one family conforms to the ideal in every area.

I want to take a moment to note something important:

While not all families are marked by severe dysfunction or unhealthy interactions, it's essential to acknowledge that certain marriages and family situations involve severe danger from physical, emotional, spiritual, or sexual abuse directed at a spouse, children, or others. Under those conditions, the emphasis on endurance, which I discuss in this book, must adapt significantly in the face of evil and immediate threats. I strongly advise against remaining in any environment where the marital vows—or familial ties—have been profoundly violated, with low prospects for secure restoration or hope of reconciliation. If this describes your reality, please reach out immediately to qualified professionals—such as counselors, clergy, law enforcement, or dedicated crisis lines—for protection and guidance without delay.

All families have their quirks, their strengths and weaknesses, their growing edges—and all are made up of imperfect people shaped by sin and grace. Every family carries a measure of brokenness, even if it looks different from household to household. As Scripture reminds us, we all "fall short of the glory of God" (Romans 3:23). I've heard it said this way, "In my own home, the only thing truly 'normal' is the setting on the dryer—and even that doesn't always work as expected." Agreed.

Perhaps that's the lesson: normal isn't the goal. Instead, grace is.

The Power of Grace

Jim and I have been married since 2003. Looking back now, it is clear that, early on, I underestimated how difficult it would be to blend our families. Our wedding photos paint a picture of a happy union, down to the giant smiles and teary eyes. However, some of those tears were not from joy; they were from fear and confusion. Our children went along with everything, seeming simultaneously excited and hesitant as we rushed all five of them into a journey they hadn't signed up for.

Not all blended families start out as messy as ours did, but even in the most thoughtfully planned, joyful, and welcomed unions, forming one propels everyone into unknown territory. As James reminds us, "you do not know what tomorrow will bring—what your life will be!" (James

4:14). While we may enter a new marriage with high hopes, we are bound to experience unforeseen challenges. Joy and heartache are frequent visitors along the path of blending. But, so is God's grace, which sustains us and invites us to grow in patience, forgiveness, and unity.

As a pastor, I take seriously the words of C. S. Lewis, "…Must we not abandon sentimental eulogies and begin to give practical advice on the high, hard, lovely, and adventurous art of really creating the Christian family?"[4] While Lewis was referring to the church, blended families are constructed in many ways. Indeed, for ours to be a channel of blessing, it must be offered to God and "converted and redeemed."[5] C.S. Lewis challenges us to move beyond sentimental ideas about family and instead embrace the hard, yet beautiful, work of genuinely creating a Christian home.

All families can reflect God's redemption, but healthy blended families spotlight it. God is committed to our family's flourishing, even in its reconstituted form. The Bible offers no perfect model; from Adam and Eve, the first dysfunctional family, the brokenness escalates. Yet, it highlights the redemptive power and healing that come through God's love, which is fulfilled in Christ. Paul reveals God's plan to adopt those of us who put our trust in Jesus into God's eternal family, through Jesus. Blended families have the potential to tangibly reflect the theological truth of spiritual adoption.

Breaking cycles of hurt is possible in Christ, but it requires intentional spiritual and emotional work to change. Thankfully, Jesus provides renewal beyond our capacity, and his constant presence supports us on the journey. It is by the power of the Holy Spirit that our family can thus become a beautiful picture of redemption, finding security in covenant relationships modeled by Jesus.

The Beatitudes and a Call to the Way of Jesus

We all want a happy family. The words of Jesus' sermon, particularly the Beatitudes and the call to action in Matthew 5:3–16, provide the theological framework for experiencing true happiness as we navigate our blended family journey with humility, mercy, peace, righteousness, and endurance. In his devotional study on the Beatitudes, the Benedictine theologian Servais Pinckaers argues that happiness is achieved not through worldly pursuits but by embracing the Beatitudes as Jesus' divine response to humanity's quest for fulfillment. Pinckaers suggests that Jesus presents the Beatitudes as paradoxical challenges and promises that transform trials—such as poverty, mourning, and persecution—into paths of spiritual freedom and grace. The way to real happiness is not found in some form of utopian ideal in this life, but in the Kingdom promised and the life to come.

In Pinckaers' own words:

> We can compare the work of the Beatitudes to that of a plow in the fields. Drawn along with determination, it drives the sharp edge of the plowshare into the earth and carves out, as the poets say, a deep wound, a broad furrow...In the same way the word of the Beatitudes penetrates us with the power of the Holy Spirit in order to break up our interior soil. It cuts through us with the sharp edge of trials and with the struggles it provokes. It overturns our ideas and projects, reverses the obvious, thwarts our desires, and bewilders us, leaving us poor and naked before God. All this, in order to prepare a place within us for the seed of new life.[6]

This perspective aligns with a deeper look at the Beatitudes' language; each of the Beatitudes begins with the Greek word *makarios* in its plural form (*makarioi*). Translators have traditionally rendered this word as "blessed," though alternatives include "fortunate," "privileged," and in some modern versions, "happy." However, I particularly favor the interpretation offered by Dr. Jonathan T. Pennington in his book *The Sermon on the Mount and Human Flourishing*. Through his meticulous analysis, he views the Beatitudes as portrayals of human "flourishing," counterintuitively derived from modest or impoverished states.[7]

Pennington warns against reading the Beatitudes as conditional or tit-for-tat statements, such as "If you do this...God will bless you."[8] Instead, he proposes them as Jesus' authoritative declaration of "what is the true way of being that will result in happiness and human flourishing."[9] He further states, "They are Jesus' answer to the universal philosophical and religious question, how can one be truly happy?"[10]

Rather than being static, our family is either growing in maturity or is in a state of decline. The Beatitudes and Jesus' call to shine our light hoists us into a mode of growth like nothing else can. We can work through the deep challenges and hurts, not by way of seeking happiness, but by banding together and keeping Christ at the center. In the way of Jesus, we and our family members can embark on a journey toward building or restoring wholeness.[11] Even the struggles along this journey become an opportunity for increased intimacy among family members and a time to draw near to God and others.

This brings me to the point of providing you with a warning and a way out. This book invites you to do some deep internal work. If you are not ready for the Lord Jesus to challenge you, stretch you, and call you to rethink your concept of what happiness can be both as individuals and corporately within your family, perhaps this book is not for you—at least not yet. I recognize that you may have picked up this book hoping for a solution to some very difficult situation in your family that has left you confused, numb, or with grief that has torn your family apart, if not your heart. Sometimes, when we're in that place of deep grief, we need another human to sit with us in our pain like Job's friends did (Job 2:11–13). If that is you, this book may not be the place to invest in...*yet.*

Think of this book as the conversation Job had with God *after* he mourned for a time and received support from others (a story told over thirty-seven chapters!). God's response, starting in Job 38, was not to respond to Job's complaints, explain, or alleviate his suffering. It was a whirlwind of rhetorical questions about the wonders of creation, highlighting God's infinite wisdom and sovereignty over the universe. The authoritative engagement and gentle rebuke served to challenge Job, reset his theology, and correct his thinking. It was a call for Job to redirect his attention from human demands for answers to divine mystery and trust.

The Beatitudes are a summary of Jesus' entire teaching and are typical of God's interactions with his people. His words humble the proud and offer grace to the humble. The Lord is always inviting us to trust him more, and we need his help to do so. In the words of Jerry Bridges, "We are responsible to trust Him in times of adversity, but we are dependent upon the Holy Spirit to enable us to do so."[12] If you are searching for "blessedness" or happiness for your family—especially amid many struggles—I pray this book offers you insight and encouragement to trust God more.

When families embrace Jesus' way of blessedness, they are poised to experience the profound transformation only Jesus can bring into their lives. Consequently, they become radiant witnesses of Christ's redeeming work and a blessing to others. I am convinced, as Paul declares, that "He who started a good work in you will carry it on to completion until the day of Christ Jesus" (Philippians 1:6).

Through biblical wisdom and practical tools, you can cultivate a healthy, united, Christ-centered family that benefits not only immediate members but also future generations and the broader community.

As we embark on this journey, remember that in Christ, your family can thrive while also reflecting his eternal, inclusive love and drawing you closer to him who holds the treasures our hearts long for. May Paul's words ring true in you and your family:

> I want their hearts to be encouraged and joined together in love, so that they may have all the riches of complete understanding and have the knowledge of God's mystery—Christ. In him are hidden all the treasures of wisdom and knowledge. (Colossians 2:2–3)

PART I.
Why Is It So Hard?

CHAPTER 1

AWARENESS

THE MESS WE INHERIT

Blessed are the poor in spirit,
for the kingdom of heaven is theirs.

—MATTHEW 5:3

Family stories are sometimes passed down with pride—and sometimes in a whisper. The ones whispered often carry the weight of hardship, pain, or unspoken struggles. My great-grandmother's story was one of those. I remember being in the basement of my grandmother's house, sitting at the feet of an old wooden chair, and looking up at my sweet great-grandmother as she ate her oatmeal breakfast. I was fascinated by her wrinkled face, but the sounds of her tongue smacking against the roof of her mouth drew my attention to her lack of teeth. I couldn't help but stare with my big brown eyes and laugh silently—and she didn't seem to mind. At barely six years old, I wondered if I would someday look like her and lose my teeth. It seemed surprisingly evident to me that her history and experiences connected with mine.

Although I know very little about my great-grandmother, I was told she was a survivor. Her lack of teeth was a small sign of the hardship she'd borne and spoke of the weight of past wounds, loss, and struggles. Still, her laughter, which was bold enough to vibrate your bones, defied her pain. My grandmother, my mother, and I continue a lineage of people marked by this woman. What I didn't realize was that I had inherited more than just the potential for dentures—I was also handed down a family history shaped by both resilience and brokenness.

Notwithstanding the wonderful memories, the list of whispered struggles casts a long shadow on our generational history. Divorce, alcoholism, abuse, division, toxic relationships, and harmful behaviors such as blame, criticism, anger, resentment, disconnection, detachment, and lack of boundaries are part of the mess I've inherited. Am I the only one with a messy story? On the contrary, if we're honest, we all know that our family histories contain aspects that are not neat and tidy.

When you dig deeply into any family, you'll uncover complexity—hidden hurts, unresolved tensions, and long-standing relational patterns passed down from one generation to the next. This is especially true in blended families, as they often do not start with a clean slate. Marriage, divorce, loss, remarriage—each chapter of a family's story adds another layer of complexity. The truth is, many of us don't realize how much history we're bringing into our new marriages until it's already affecting the present.

Dysfunction Hidden in Plain Sight

The famous first line of Leo Tolstoy's novel *Anna Karenina* reads, "All happy families are alike; each unhappy family is unhappy in its own way."[1] Some have embraced this statement, dubbing it the "Anna Karenina principle," which holds that there is only one way to succeed: avoiding all the possible routes to failure.[2] Applying this principle to the context of family is discouraging. For families like mine, marked by so many whispered struggles, this idea feels overwhelming. How can any of us avoid all failure? In challenging seasons, moments of doubt, and especially amid our messy reality, it's easy to believe that only a flawless family dynamic brings happiness.

Still, we know better: happy families do exist, each wonderfully diverse and somewhat flawed. Tolstoy's words suggest that happiness follows a predictable pattern, while dysfunction and hardship manifest differently in every family. Happy families indeed thrive on common elements such as physical health, financial stability, and mutual affection. Yet even with all these "happy" factors in place, every family has its messy side—whether visible or hidden.

No family, not even the happiest, escapes some level of dysfunction.

We often believe that other families have it all together while ours feels utterly chaotic. Yet, in reality, every home encounters its own challenges. Despite the smiles in photos, the laughter at gatherings, and the appearance of genuinely enjoying each other's company, a more complex story unfolds beneath the surface and behind the walls of every home. I've spent much of my adult life in the work of ministry, and perhaps that's given me more opportunity than most to see this truth firsthand.

We may not recognize that a family struggles with personality differences, disagreements, disappointments, unresolved past hurts, toxic patterns, ingratitude, emotional wounds, and even grief unless they choose to share it. Such discussions are typically reserved for private reflections or a circle of trusted individuals. This doesn't mean the family is irreparably broken; rather, it means every family is composed of real people, each with their own struggles. Every family is unique in its experience, even if they share much in common with others.

Gabor Maté, in *The Myth of Normal.* challenges the assumption that dysfunction is an exception rather than the rule. He argues that "much of what passes for normal in our society is neither healthy nor natural."[3]

Our emotional and relational struggles are not just personal—they are shaped by cultural expectations, family dynamics, and even past generations' unprocessed pain.

Maté claims that our dysfunction is often hidden in plain sight. Early life experiences shape our health and behavior, underscoring the need to recognize and address intergenerational trauma within families. In his book, he emphasizes that denial is the number one obstacle to receiving healing.

Okay, to heal, we must face our dysfunction. But can we identify what it is?

Is My Family Dysfunctional?

While there is no strict definition of a "dysfunctional family," this phrase is a catch-all for a family suffering from a myriad of relational struggles. Healthcare professionals define a dysfunctional family as one "in which relationships or communication are impaired, and members are unable to attain closeness and self-expression,"[4] or "one where relationships among family members are not conducive to emotional and physical health."[5]

A dysfunctional family doesn't have to be abusive or chaotic to carry wounds. At its core, dysfunction refers to relational patterns such as constant criticism, lack of affection, unclear roles, avoidance of hard conversations, or unspoken resentments. Sometimes dysfunction is loud and obvious—other times, it hides in silence. What matters is not how visible the pain is, but how it shapes our sense of identity, safety, and love within our home.

A dysfunctional family is plagued by immature behavior, emotional, psychological, and spiritual impairment, and unhealthy codependent or toxic connections that bring harm to one or more individuals within the family. On the other hand, a functional family exhibits mature behavior, healthy emotional, psychological, and spiritual growth, and confidence in individuality while remaining connected and supportive of others.

It's essential to recognize that family dysfunction exists on a spectrum. Every family faces challenges, but the degree and impact of those struggles vary significantly. Some families experience deep fractures caused by trauma, violence, or severe instability—realities that shape every aspect of their lives. Others navigate more subtle but still painful relational issues, such as unresolved conflict, poor communication, or emotional distance. Is there dysfunction in your family? As a Christian who is well-aware of the reality of human brokenness due to sin, I'd say, "Yes!" However, having dysfunction in your family is not the same thing as being a dysfunctional family.

Think of it this way: just as every human body experiences occasional aches, pains, or minor illnesses—none of us are perfectly healthy all the time—it doesn't mean the body as a whole is chronically ill or unable to function. Similarly, dysfunction in a family refers to specific areas of imperfection or challenge that arise from our shared human brokenness. A dysfunctional family, on the other hand, implies a pervasive pattern.

In preparing to write this book, I've noticed that we're prone to say, with a tinge of humor, something like, "Every family is dysfunctional." This is unfortunate. I don't believe it's wise to paint every family with the broad brush of dysfunction. All families occasionally struggle with disagreements, conflict, and personality issues. To some extent, it is a mark of a healthy family that these exist.

Saying that *all* families are dysfunctional can oversimplify the issue, minimizing the suffering of those in extreme situations while overlooking the reality that some families, though imperfect, provide stability, love, and security. Acknowledging these differences allows us to approach family brokenness with both truth and compassion.

Regardless of the level of dysfunction, it is often intergenerational, passed down from one generation to the next. Sadly, it appears to be the most widely accepted form of inheritance. However, overcoming inherited dysfunction is possible, especially when we understand the role of individual choices and faith in transforming family dynamics.[6] More on this later. But, for now, I want you to rest in this truth: we can identify unhealthy patterns and increase our reliance on biblical principles, thus healing and establishing healthy relationships.

Don't worry. You're not alone, and as imperfect as it might be, your family isn't hopeless. While we can't control every outcome in our families, we can choose to grow in health. This is why I intend to offer you practical tips and resources to encourage and help you.

However, before we proceed, remember that while learning communication tools, attending family counseling, or reading books on stepparenting are valuable and practical ways to move toward health, no technique can guarantee transformation. No strategy can guarantee peace. You cannot control people's behavior. That's why we don't just need information and strategies—we need Jesus.

Jesus doesn't promise us perfect families, but he promises us his presence. And it's His grace that ultimately changes us from the inside out, allowing love to grow even in imperfect soil. That is why I agree with Maté that we must face our condition and connection with every other family head-on, not exaggerate it or minimize it, and find freedom from the tendency to think our family is either the worst or must be flawless.

Dysfunction Isn't New; It's as Old as Humanity

If a family pretends to be perfect, their pretense flies in the face of the human brokenness the Bible so bluntly reveals: "There is certainly no one righteous on earth who does good and never sins" (Ecclesiastes 7:20), "for all have sinned and fall short of the glory of God" (Romans 3:23).

There's a reason family sitcoms are widely popular: they resonate with a universal experience.

Despite the current attention, dysfunction (no matter its form) is not a modern phenomenon. From Adam and Eve's fall to the dysfunction seen in biblical families to that in our families today, humanity's brokenness is woven into our family stories. Patterns of shame, blame, and unresolved conflict ripple through generations, shaping how we love, react, and connect.

It's reassuring that biblical families struggled just as ours do. In their book *Flawed Families of the Bible*, authors David and Diana Garland explore the complex and often dysfunctional family narratives within the Bible. They introduce their book with this fact: "The stories of families in the Bible are raw and uncensored, bitter reminders of how awful family life can become."[7] From the first pages of the Bible, we are invited into the "living rooms" of our faith patriarchs to see played out the issues of family dynamics: sibling rivalry, marital challenges, infertility, and, yes, blended family complexities. These ancient stories are relevant to us today and inform how we think about our own families. They also offer us comfort and guidance as we face similar issues.

To me, Genesis 4 resembles the "CliffsNotes" version of family dysfunction. It serves as a compressed narrative of the human family's condition and God's grace, encapsulating both the beauty of hope and the devastating reality of sin. The first family, consisting of two parents and two sons, begins with the promise of new life.

Cain and Abel, the first children born into the world, symbolize the potential for renewal after their parents', Adam and Eve, fall in the garden. Yet, this hope quickly unravels as jealousy, pride, and unchecked anger enter the picture. It is here that we witness dysfunction in its most deadly form. Cain, envious of Abel's favor with God, allows his resentment to fester, leading to the first act of human violence—brother killing brother.

This tragic turn reveals how sin corrupts relationships at their core. What should have been a bond of love between siblings becomes fractured by comparison and competition. Cain's defiance when confronted by God—*"Am I my brother's guardian?"* (Genesis 4:9)—echoes throughout history as humanity struggles with selfishness, relational brokenness, and a refusal to take responsibility for one another. Yet, even in this tragic account, God's justice and mercy are evident.

Though Cain's actions warrant punishment, God places a mark of protection on him, preventing others from taking revenge. This moment foreshadows God's enduring grace. Despite our failures, He does not abandon us.

Genesis 4 is not just an ancient story; it is a mirror reflecting the struggles within every family, every human heart. Sin patterns repeat across generations. We all wrestle with jealousy, anger, and the temptation to justify our wrongdoing. This is true in blended families as well as unblended families. And yet, even in our brokenness, God calls us to something greater: to recognize our responsibility toward one another, to turn away from sin, and to trust in His redemptive mercy.

The stories in the Bible "are vital to our understanding God, our faith, ourselves, and the world."[8] The overarching presence of God's grace to biblical families reminds us that we can be honest about our struggles and failures. Abraham and Sarah, Jacob and Esau, and David and his children are not idealized family models but rather portraits of real families with genuine flaws.

God's grace is not hindered by human shortcomings. Instead, it often manifests most profoundly amidst imperfection. This should encourage us to find solace and guidance in our own familial situations, understanding that flaws do not preclude the possibility of experiencing God's transformative love and blessing. And, as we see in the tragic story of Cain and Abel, Scripture doesn't only give us diagnoses; it offers us glimpses of grace. I saw one of those glimpses in my own childhood.

Flowers from the Mess

As a single mother raising seven children, my mother didn't have the resources for expensive outings. When I was nine, six of us moved with her from Puerto Rico to the South Bronx in New York. It was a very difficult time for our family. My teenage brothers, missing a father figure, argued and fought regularly with each other and my mom. My younger brother struggled and misbehaved in school, and every day, my mother disciplined him more harshly than she would later say she should have. My sister experienced harassment and trauma every day after school at the hands of a group of mean girls, but none of us knew how to help her. Deep wounds of fear injured her soul even as her muscles grew strong from miles of running away from her chasers.

Our tiny one-bedroom apartment was too small to contain the ballooning emotions and wounds that arose when we were all inside during the weekends. So, my mother came up with a brilliant idea. Early Saturday morning, we embarked on our dollar-each, full-day train ride, our backpacks filled with drinks, lunch, and snacks. We took up an entire row and spent the day people-watching, playing silly games, and making faces. Our loud, joyous peels of laughter rang out, turning a long, boring metro train ride into something fun. The train car was not bigger than our apartment, but inspired by our mother's creativity, we transformed a usually miserable experience into something that I think entertained— dare I say, blessed—all of us and the other passengers.

My mother found a way to turn something mundane—riding the train—into a source of joy. Looking back, I realize that she was showing us something deeper: that even in difficult circumstances, we can find a blessing—even if it's just one bright moment amidst a hard life. She couldn't change our circumstances, but she could change how we experienced them. She was present and attentive to our needs. When we place our circumstances in God's hands, something as ordinary as a train ride can be transformed.

God's grace works in much the same way. The families we meet in Scripture were far from perfect. They're riddled with betrayal, jealousy, and dysfunction. Yet, over and over, we see that God is still at work amongst them, redeeming what is broken and leading them to a flourishing life.

That kind of flourishing is still available for blended (and unblended) families today.

Reorienting Our Thinking and Heart

Jonathan T. Pennington notes that through the Beatitudes, Jesus invites us to "reorient our thinking and sensibilities about what it means to thrive and live fully."[9] This means reshaping not just our thoughts but also our deepest feelings and assumptions about true blessing. This is not easily done. In Matthew 5:3, when Jesus said, "Blessed are the poor in spirit, for the kingdom of heaven is theirs," we are challenged to see this as plausible. True blessing, it turns out, is not about worldly security or achieving perfection but about learning to depend on God in our poverty—whether financial, emotional, relational, or spiritual.

Pennington observes that this is the "darkness" of the Beatitudes, that "what Jesus proclaims as being a state of flourishing includes many things that humanity naturally and even vehemently seeks to avoid," such as poverty of spirit.[10] The poor are often found in the lower echelons of society. How is it possible that they possess God's Kingdom? Because God is their faithful provider.

Jesus invites us into a posture of surrender and humility, one that acknowledges our deep need for him. Yet this Beatitude is saying more than that. It claims that in the state of poverty, amid the suffering and waiting for God's action, we can experience flourishing. Accepting the reality of our blended family's brokenness is not about dwelling in shame or despair, but about recognizing that we cannot fix it completely by ourselves. Whether deep wounds or everyday struggles mark our dysfunction, we are all spiritually impoverished apart from Christ, and only he has the power to transform.

The good news is that Jesus does not turn away from our mess; he steps into it. His Kingdom is not for those who have it all together, but for those who admit they don't. When we bring our family histories, relational failures, and personal shortcomings before Jesus, we are not met with condemnation but with the promise of redemption. Through Jesus alone, our stories are rewritten—not into flawlessness, but into flourishing shaped by his grace, love, and faithfulness.

God can work in your family in so many ways, big and small. Perhaps, in his kindness, he can increase our sense of humor. As my friend, Samantha, who herself is dealing with merged family struggles, likes to say, "Laughter can heal a broken moment." It can also build positive experiences and memories. Our family nickname, *Smoothie*, is an expression of our eagerness to laugh often, to not take ourselves too seriously, and to leave room for some silliness. By sharing funny memes in our group text chat or laughing at Papa's jokes at the dinner table, even though we've heard them a thousand times, we weave memories of joy into the fabric of our family history.

Appropriate humor in painful situations can also be cathartic because it offers a momentary release from emotional tension. Even a silent laugh, like the one I offered my great-grandmother, can foster connection and resilience without diminishing the gravity of the struggle. Her teeth weren't coming back, but she could still smile, and I was smiling with her.

That train ride will forever be, for me, a reminder of just how poor we were. But it is also a reminder that blessings aren't always found in what I have—they're found in the One whose Kingdom is not of this world. My mother showed us that poverty, whether financial or spiritual, doesn't have to be the end of the story. If you are experiencing poverty in your own family—be it relational, emotional, or physical poverty—it is not the end of your story either. This, too, is at the heart of Matthew 5:3. Jesus calls blessed those who have no choice but to recognize their need...those who understand that they can't do it on their own.

Looking back, I see how that experience foreshadowed my deeper spiritual journey—learning that in our moments of need, lack, and brokenness, we still can flourish in the redemption and blessing of God. He doesn't always change our circumstances immediately, or at all, but he invites us to live them through his grace—turning what feels like brokenness into something that ultimately points us and others to his glory.

As we continue in this book, we will see how, with the help of Jesus, intergenerational dysfunction and trauma can be broken. It doesn't have to be passed down. While our family may not reach perfection, and neither will we, individually, until Jesus returns or takes us home, we can certainly be agents of generational healing and abundant blessings by the power of the Holy Spirit.

Acknowledging dysfunction, to whatever extent it may be present, is the first step toward healing. Still, simply naming our struggles isn't enough—we need something greater than ourselves. This is why the gospel is such good news for families. Through Christ, generational cycles can be broken, wounds can be healed, and new legacies can be formed—even in blended families. As we embark on this journey of healing, may we remember the words of the psalmist: "Unless the Lord builds a house, its builders labor over it in vain" (Psalm 127:1a).

PRACTICAL TOOLS:

- **Self-Reflection Exercise**: Draw your family tree, including at least three generations, starting with your grandparents and continuing to the youngest generation. Note key patterns of relational dynamics. Use lines, symbols, and brief notes to indicate relational dynamics (divorce, closeness, conflict, or estrangement). This is what is called a "genogram." Once your genogram is complete, mentally put yourself in the shoes of another family member. What might it feel like to be like them? How might their experiences have shaped their actions?

- **Healing Discussion:** Identify and discuss past patterns or wounds that may still impact your current family relationships. Without judgment, state what has been passed down in your family, good and bad.

- **Prayer Prompt:** Confession. Write down areas of brokenness or struggle within your family and bring them to God in prayer.

- **Beatitudes Reflection:** Reflect on Matthew 5:3 and discuss or journal about how it applies to your family relationships.

CHAPTER 2

EMPATHY

WHEN THE PAST AFFECTS THE PRESENT

Blessed are those who mourn,
for they will be comforted.

—MATTHEW 5:4

One of the joys of writing a book is receiving feedback from readers. Sometimes, however, that feedback can surprise you and lead you on a journey of discovery. After releasing my book *Uncharted,*[*] I received an unexpected kind of feedback. Readers expressed sorrow for the "trauma" they sensed in my story. This surprised me and raised my curiosity. Yes, I was raised by a single mother after divorce, endured a difficult upbringing in poverty without a relationship with my father, experienced two divorces of my own, and faced more heartache than I ever anticipated—but I hadn't named it "trauma." I didn't think of myself that way. It became clear to me that I was oblivious to the trauma I had inherited, experienced, or caused.

Evan and Jenny Owens write that "trauma is tricky; it hides in the dark and trips us up when we least expect it. It plays dirty. It tries to convince

---

[*] My book *Uncharted: Navigating Your Unique Journey of Faith* (Austin: TX, Fedd Books, 2023) is about thriving on the journey of faith. It includes my personal testimony as well as stories of people in the Bible who also struggled at times along their journeys of faith.

us that what we experienced was normal and to minimize and excuse it while stacking itself up against someone else who 'had it worse.'"[1] This must have been my mindset.

After all, I hadn't been diagnosed with depression, anxiety, chronic illness, phobias, obsessive thoughts, PTSD, or other debilitating conditions. Psychologists view these as signs that a person may have experienced or inherited family trauma.[2] I wasn't frozen by fear or overtaken by grief. But looking back, I see now: the words in my book leaked the pain in my heart. I had buried wounds so deeply that even I couldn't see them. And like many who grew up in challenging environments, I overperformed—perhaps in an effort to prove the past had no power over me.

All blended families have experienced wounds of one kind or another. They are formed after either a divorce, a death, or the dissolution of a serious relationship. All of these things involve fracture. Think of a tree that has had a limb broken off. It doesn't necessarily imply any fault in the tree. It does, however, mean that something has broken and that healing must occur if the tree is to continue a healthy life.

What Is Trauma?

Trauma has become a popular subject and a catch-all for many human experiences. It seems everyone is traumatized these days. Have we over diagnosed ourselves and others?* Gabor Maté describes what trauma is and what it is not. Trauma, according to Maté, is "not what happens to you but what happens inside you."[3] He uses the example of a car accident to differentiate between the collision and the lasting consequences. Trauma is a "psychic injury" that lasts long past the event that caused it. He writes,

---

* With trauma becoming a common label for all sorts of experiences, it's worth keeping in mind there are ongoing debates between the experts, including those quoted in this book.

It is the constellation of hardships, composed of the wound itself and the residual burdens that our woundedness imposes on our bodies and souls: the unresolved emotions they visit upon us; the coping dynamics they dictate; the tragic melodramatic or neurotic scripts we unwittingly but inexorably live out; and not least, the toll these take on our bodies.[4]

Maté describes trauma as an open sore, a raw wound or scar that hasn't healed, easily injured again by the "slightest stimulus," and causing us to remain ever-diligent in keeping it from awakening. Such trauma, the type that involves automatic responses and forces the mind and body to maladapt to our environment, impedes our flourishing until we work through it. Trauma can come in two forms. One which Maté calls "big-*T* trauma" refers to experiences such as severe abuse, severe neglect, racism, or oppression—"when things happen to vulnerable people that should *not* have happened."[5] The other, which he calls "small-*t* trauma," refers to being wounded in multiple lesser ways, but also to good things not happening. It encompasses the long-lasting effect of ordinary events that are hurtful.[6]

What Do We Do with Our Family Trauma and Pain?

According to leading experts in psychology and neurobiology, the body has its own memory. Trauma, particularly family trauma, doesn't disappear simply because we ignore it. It seeks to be acknowledged and processed. Even trauma experienced by our family members, known or unknown, can be stored in our bodies through the epigenetic process,*[7] imprinted in our emotions, and echoed in our relationships—passed down through generations like an unwelcome heirloom.[8] Wolynn contends that "unconsciously,

---

* *Epigenetics is the study of changes in gene function that are heritable and that do not entail a change in DNA sequence.*

we could find ourselves reacting to certain people, events, or situations in old, familiar ways that echo the past."[9] We often just accept this kind of inherited family pain, and Maté refers to this as the "myth of normal"—the assumption that just because something is common (such as family dysfunction or emotional distance), it's healthy. However, as I have already noted, "normal" doesn't mean whole.

Even therapy, which is often a pathway to healing, must be pursued wisely. As Abigail Shrier cautions in *Bad Therapy*, sometimes well-meaning interventions can worsen things, especially if they encourage us to dwell in victimhood rather than move toward growth. Other experts offer this sobering warning: *"Grief is about a broken heart, not a broken brain. All efforts to heal the heart with the head fail because the head is the wrong tool for the job. It's like trying to paint with a hammer—it only makes a mess."*[10] Still, healing is possible—but it begins with telling the truth. Time is not always the healer we expect it to be; action may be necessary.

And that's where Matthew 5:4 meets us: "Blessed are those who mourn..."

Mourning isn't just about grieving the death of a loved one. It includes grieving what we never had—a stable home, a faithful parent, a healthy marriage. It pours out from the sorrow of unmet expectations, broken promises, and fractured relationships. In blended families, especially, these wounds are often complicated. Some are visible, while others are buried beneath the surface. Mourning invites us to stop pretending everything is fine and instead bring our old and new pain before God.

Here too, the words of Servais Pinckaers seem apropos:

Among all the Beatitudes there is none like this one for flying in the face of common sense. No one believes that happiness is the lot of those who weep and mourn. We all spontaneously associate happiness with joy, laughter, and the pleasures of life...So what are we to make of this beatitude of mourning and tears? Shouldn't it be revised to fit contemporary needs and ideas?... Shouldn't we fight suffering and death, instead of accepting them passively?"[11]

Jesus doesn't shame us for grieving. We are blessed because he is with us in it.

When we have the courage to allow ourselves to mourn, we make room for God to comfort us—not with quick fixes or trite advice, but with his presence, which offers us deep, healing, redemptive comfort. As 2 Corinthians 1:3–7 tells us, he is the "Father of mercies and the God of all comfort," who comforts us in our troubles *so that* we can comfort others in theirs. Our mourning becomes a fertile ground for ministry to grow—a path to healing not just for us, but for our family. In our familial relationships, where layers of grief can pile up unacknowledged, our willingness to mourn can be the most redemptive gift we give.

The past Has Power, but It Doesn't Have to Define the Future

The past has a way of shaping the present, sometimes through unhealed wounds, unspoken expectations, or deep-seated patterns passed down through generations. Blended families often carry the weight of past relationships and bear the scars from prior marriages, betrayals, disappointments, and losses. It's the kind of grief that doesn't get a funeral, but it constructs its own tombstone. Children may carry confusion, resentment, and unspoken fears, unsure of their place in a reshaped home. Parents often operate out of guilt, shame, or the pressure to pretend that everything is going to be great or "back to normal." While they didn't sign up for it, stepparents often feel the sting of rejection despite their sincere love and effort. It is difficult for a family to move forward while old wounds linger just beneath the surface. These unacknowledged griefs create emotional distance and relational strain unless they are named, mourned, and surrendered.

Grief is a necessary part of healing, but it is not where we should stay.

Mourning makes room for grace. It clears away the clutter of resentment, denial, and suppression. It allows us to say, "this is hard, this hurts, and this matters." Only then can we begin to receive the comfort of Christ and invite others into that space. In her book, *Break the Cycle*, Dr. Mariel Buqué reminds us that trauma is not just inherited biologically or emotionally.[12] It shapes how we see ourselves, how we connect with others, and how we build or rebuild our families. But just as trauma can be passed down, so can healing. Healing is not accidental. It is chosen. And it begins with honesty.

The Hard Part of Mourning: Forgiveness

Forgiveness, too, is a part of mourning. When we forgive, to whatever extent we can, we are not simply "moving on." We are embodying the very heart of the gospel—extending grace as we've received it.

Forgiveness is not a passive act of "forgetting or whitewashing the other person's bad behavior"[13] but rather an active choice to release or let go of what you cannot change, making space for what God can redeem. As Dr. Harriet Lerner articulately states, "Letting go means protecting ourselves from the corrosive effects of staying stuck." Studies have shown that unforgiveness keeps the body in a state of chronic stress, resulting in increased levels of hormones like cortisol, which can lead to inflammation, high blood pressure, and weakened immunity. Over time, this unresolved tension can result in anxiety, fatigue, and even physical pain, as the body retains what the heart refuses to release. This is why genuine healing necessitates courage, not control.

Forgiveness is perhaps the most expensive gift we can offer another person. It costs us our sense of justice because we let go of the demand that the other person "make it right" or suffer as we have. It costs us our pride because we choose to release our right to be right. It costs us our control because we surrender the power that resentment gives us over someone else. And most profoundly, it costs us our pain because to truly forgive, we must honestly face the wound without minimizing it, and choose to release it instead of using it to define ourselves. Forgiveness is not cheap. It doesn't erase the past or dismiss the wrong. But it is profoundly Christlike because it mirrors what Jesus has done for us. He didn't just let go or minimize the consequences of our actions. By his love, Jesus secured our blessedness. John writes, "Love consists in this: not that we loved God, but that he loved us and sent his Son to be the atoning sacrifice for our sins" (1 John 4:10).

As the most significant expression of his love, Jesus paid the highest price to forgive our sins—not with words alone, but with his life.* We echo that kind of radical love when we forgive. even the unforgivable, the most heinous acts, and the most horrific of situations. It's costly, yes, but it's also the path to our Christlikeness.

Mourning And Forgiveness Take Time

That said, rushing into forgiveness may not actually rid us of anger, bitterness, resentment, and pain. In blended families, wounds may come from many directions: former spouses, co-parenting dynamics, or even our spouse and the children themselves. Their history is layered, and wounds run deep. Forgiveness may be the hardest step, one that takes time and

---

* A sampling of Bible verses about Jesus dying on the cross for our sins: Romans 5:8, Philippians 2:5–11, 1 Peter 2:24, 1 John 4:7–16.

intentionality, but it's also the most healing because it helps us experience resolution, moving on, and letting go in the most profound manner. Grace is needed on every side.

I found this to be true in my own family. Jim and I brought together five children in the most unconventional way—a manner I would not recommend to anyone—but one that I trust the Lord has redeemed by his mercy. If you have read my book *Uncharted* or ever listened to much of my public speaking, you know that we started our relationship in an extramarital affair. I was a twice-divorced woman with a son from my first marriage and two daughters from my second; Jim was married and had two daughters. We worked together for many years and entered a romantic relationship after my second divorce, at a time when his marriage was in crisis. Neither one of us was walking with the Lord. Jim considered himself Christian-lite, and I was agnostic. What we did was wrong, and our actions caused immense pain to the people we love, including our children, and even to ourselves. After Jim's divorce, we married and began the journey of our blended family, marked by our shared wounds. Together, we started following the Lord Jesus. Grace and forgiveness flooded our daily prayers. It took all of us to lean into Christlike love and to connect us as we are today. It is a wonder and a miracle that, as of this writing, our family is unified, and a great deal of healing has occurred since we started our journey twenty-four years ago.

If our story can be redeemed, so can yours. No beginning is too broken for God's mercy to rewrite.

Scripture reminds us of this truth—that no family is beyond redemption.* Shaping the present and future toward a healthier family dynamic is achievable. We can acknowledge our vulnerability and painful experiences

---

* The gospel offers not just individual redemption but also the restoration of relationships, including family. God's grace is abundant and wise enough to restore even our deepest relational wounds. Redemption doesn't erase the pain, but it transforms the outcome. God doesn't discard what is broken but rebuilds it into something glorious. See for example: Ephesians 1:7–8, Genesis 50:20, Deuteronomy 31:8, Isaiah 61:3.

without allowing them to dictate the future. Healing requires the courage to grieve and forgive, the grace to let go of resentment, and the faith to trust that God wastes nothing—not even our most challenging moments. When we surrender our past to Jesus, we not only unearth buried hurt but also discover unexpected treasures of healing, unity, and redemption.

So, where do we begin?

We begin by acknowledging that though grief doesn't always announce itself, it still needs to be named, felt, and healed. We begin by telling the truth. By sitting with our sorrow, not rushing it, and by seeking God's healing. By writing a letter we may never send. By crying the tears we've tucked away for years. By opening our hearts to God's healing compassion. We begin by allowing ourselves to mourn the things we've lost, even if they were never ours to begin with. And as we mourn, we invite Jesus into the space where we were once alone. Because "blessed are those who mourn, for they will be comforted." And when God's love and presence comfort us, we become agents of comfort to others, particularly within our families. Through this healing, we create a nurturing environment for the next generation. When we invite Jesus into our mourning, we become a safe space where our children, too, can mourn and find solace.

Because some sorrows don't come with ceremonies, consider creating small, symbolic rituals—lighting a candle, journaling a prayer, or holding a family discussion—to acknowledge what's been lost, invite God's comfort, and celebrate what has been redeemed.

PRACTICAL TOOLS:

- **Self-Reflection Exercise:** Revisit the genogram you created at the end of Chapter 1. Identify any unresolved trauma and take a step toward mourning and resolution. Write a "Letter of Release"—a letter you may never send—to acknowledge and release past hurt. Name what you lost. Name what you longed for. Notice God's presence in that space.

- **Healing Discussion:** Write down your greatest joy and greatest struggle in your family. Share it with a trusted loved one or counselor. How have these shaped your faith?

- **Prayer Prompt:** Ask God to help you identify where the past—yours or someone else's in your family history—is affecting your current relationships. Pray for the courage to mourn, forgive, and move forward.

- **Beatitudes Reflection:** Reflect on Matthew 5:4 and 2 Corinthians 1:3–7. How has God comforted you in the past? How might he be inviting you to receive and extend comfort now, especially within your family?

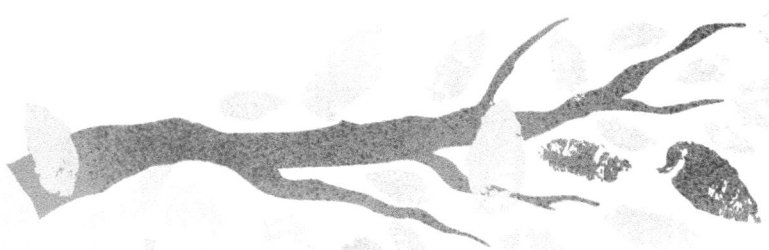

CHAPTER 3

HOPE

CHANGING FAMILY ROLES AND UNMET EXPECTATIONS

Blessed are the humble,
for they will inherit the earth.

—MATTHEW 5:5

As I prepared to officiate the ceremony and host the celebration of my son's marriage in our backyard this spring, I was surrounded by the vibrant blooms of pink, red, and purple flowers—colors his fiancée chose to reflect their deep, joyful love. The scent of fresh orange blossoms mingled with the warm April breeze, and my heart swelled with anticipation for the joy of their covenantal union, the laughter we were about to share, and the sacred beauty of this family-only gathering. Yet, with stepparents, stepsiblings, and half-siblings from multiple marriages coming together, this celebration wasn't just a wedding—it was a testament to God's redemptive work in our messy, beautiful story. In the spirit of Matthew 5:5, "Blessed are the humble, for they will inherit the earth," I was reminded that humility has been the quiet strength guiding us through decades of challenges, leading us to this moment of healing and hope.

Reflecting on my son's journey to his wedding day, I remembered him as the lanky teenager with a quiet smirk when Jim and I married. For years, he wrestled with ADHD challenges, which only intensified as he navigated adolescence and faced the big questions boys often face, like "Who am I?" His identity was still forming, and his body was morphing into that of a man. Sadly, the shifting foundation of our family became like quicksand beneath his sense of self. Without a stable notion of who he was and how he belonged, his identity seemed to slip into the unknown. In the turmoil of my shattered marriage and the arrival of a new family, his struggle deepened, and in his own words, "he learned to drift...go with the flow...numb out to manage."

Already, he had two half-sisters from my second marriage and a half-brother and half-sister from his father's second marriage. My third marriage brought two older stepsisters into his life, upending the dynamics he'd once known. Overnight, he went from being the oldest to the middle child, a shift that left him unmoored. I didn't fully grasp how deeply he was struggling, nor how my second divorce had compounded his pain, making addictive substances an attractive place to secretly escape and cope. One afternoon, I found him in the bathroom, the sharp scent of marijuana cutting through the air, his eyes red, not just from the smoke but from tears. "What do you expect me to do, Mom?" he snapped, his voice cracking with raw pain. "I'm trying to deal with this nightmare." In that moment, I saw the weight of my choices reflected in his anger—the way my decisions to divorce and remarry had reshaped his world, leaving him to grapple with a question that haunted him: *Am I also disposable?* My heart sank with a mix of guilt and helplessness, knowing I'd played a role in his suffering, yet unsure how to bridge the gap between us.

The inherited dysfunctions and traumas we discussed in the previous chapters are not the only factors that make blended family experiences so challenging. We do not grow up in isolation. The patterns, expectations, and roles within our families shape our beliefs, habits, and sense of belonging. Roles often shift when we reconstitute a family, sometimes painfully, and as new relationships form, old dynamics are redefined. Changes in birth order may present difficulties for children and affect their development.[1] An additional complication arises as the family adjusts to the new familial structure. A child who once held a specific position in the family may suddenly feel displaced, grieving the loss of familiarity and struggling to find their place. Often, these events spark conflict, resentment, disunity, and explosive emotions within family interactions, and they can take us by surprise, even though they shouldn't.

Family Systems Shape Us

In *The Hidden Life of Trees*,[2] Peter Wohlleben offers a captivating exploration of how trees live, grow, and interact with each other in ways that mirror the social structures of animals and even humans. Drawing from groundbreaking scientific research and his own experience as a forester in Germany, Wohlleben reveals that trees communicate through underground fungal networks (sometimes called the "wood wide web"), support weaker neighbors, warn each other of danger, and even grieve the loss of companions. His accessible and poetic writing invites readers to see trees not as static plants but as dynamic, interconnected beings. The book challenges us to rethink our understanding of nature and encourages a deeper respect for forests as living communities. The back cover of the book reads:

> ...trees are like human families: tree parents live together with their children, communicate with them, support them as they grow, share nutrients with those who are sick or struggling, and even warn each other of impending dangers.

By scientifically comparing a network of trees to a human family, Wohlleben gives us a fresh perspective on the life of woods and forests by revealing the social network that helps them thrive. If trees are this interconnected, how much more are we, created in God's image and in the likeness of a relational God?[3] Unlike trees, human beings are profoundly emotionally driven creatures. Our families are emotional ecosystems, shaping us in profound ways. When my son lashed out that day in the bathroom, I began to see how deeply the changes in our family system had influenced him.

Family systems act as the primary environment where we first learn patterns of behavior, communication, and relational dynamics. According to family systems theory, pioneered by psychiatrist Murray Bowen, families are interconnected units where each member's actions influence the others.[4] Our family shapes us in four key ways:

1. It teaches us how to handle emotions, whether through direct expression, suppression, or avoidance. In our home, we often avoided conflict, which may have left my son ill-equipped to voice his struggles.*

2. It also assigns us roles within the family that can persist into adulthood (e.g., caretaker, peacemaker, rebel), influencing how we interact in other systems, such as work or friendships. My son, once the oldest sibling, had his role stripped away when my third marriage added two older stepsisters.

3. Patterns, even pain, pass down through generations—my own fears of failure as a mother likely echoed in my son's sense of self.[5]

---

* A family that openly discusses feelings might foster emotional intelligence, while one that avoids conflict could lead to difficulties in assertiveness later in life. Research by Bowen highlights how "differentiation of self"—the ability to separate one's emotions from the family's—impacts personal resilience and relationships.

4. And we learn by watching, absorbing how to trust or argue from those around us.[6] Albert Bandura's social learning theory supports this, showing that children learn behaviors by observing and imitating family members—and that those behaviors are reinforced through reward and punishment. My son, likely, learned resilience and self-reliance from watching me navigate trust issues rooted in my father's absence, while also seeing the strength it took to build a new family.

Studies show that supportive families foster better mental health, while high-conflict ones can lead to challenges like depression.[7] But adaptability—flexibility in roles and rules—helps us thrive through change. For my son, the complexity of our family magnified these dynamics, making his journey to healing both harder and, ultimately, more redemptive. As I reflected on this while I prepared for his wedding, I saw how those early struggles shaped him and how his willingness to articulate his feelings planted seeds for the unity we celebrated that weekend.

Shifting Dynamics

The wedding guest list told the story of our family's complicated nature: my son's father and stepmother, his first stepfather and wife, Jim and me, his four half-siblings, two stepsisters and their families, and his bride's loved ones, all gathered in our backyard. With only fifty people, the seating chart still felt like a puzzle—until my son and his wife opted for a sweetheart table and open seating, letting love guide the mingling. This wedding marks my son's second marriage, and with my daughter-in-law and his boys, he's stepping into a new family dynamic, one that will again reshape the underground emotional connections we share. I pray the lessons we've learned—patience, grace, and humility—will guide him as he builds his new family.

Blending a family always brings challenges, amplifying the ways family systems shape us. The emotional turbulence can be intense—loyalty conflicts, grief over past losses, and resistance to new roles often surface. My son felt this deeply when Jim and I married, his loyalty to his father and first stepfather clashing with his uncertainty about Jim's place in his life. It took years for our *Smoothie* to find unity. The journey has taught us what psychologists have noted through research and clinical work: trust builds slowly amid competing loyalties, and individuals in blended families often face a longer path to emotional integration.[8] Jim and I have witnessed this play out in our family, especially as our five children came together in their teenage years and each enjoyed a strong bond with their biological parents. Thanks to everyone's effort, lots of prayer, and God-given patience, our family found connection, trust, and unity.

Roles in these merged families can be ambiguous or contested, creating emotional complexity. A stepparent might struggle to balance being a disciplinarian with feeling like an outsider, while stepsiblings may compete for attention or parental favor. Emphasis on boundaries, as Salvador Minuchin points out, is critical in these dynamics.[9] Families with undefined boundaries (e.g., a stepparent overstepping into a co-parent's domain) can experience increased tension. In contrast, families that establish flexible yet firm boundaries early on experience less role confusion and increased harmony.

Finding your way in this minefield of emotions is not easy, but it's possible. My son went from oldest to middle child, a loss that fueled his teenage sense of displacement. Clear boundaries helped. Early on, Jim and I established a hierarchy: God first, then our marriage, then our children (while honoring their biological parents), and finally others. This framework provided stability and helped us navigate moments of tension. Though Jim and I sometimes felt overwhelmed by the competing demands and emotional complexities of our family, we found beauty and potential for growth in working through them together.

Merging households provides a rich environment for learning, especially when healthy boundaries are established. Dr. Henry Cloud and Dr. John Townsend contend that establishing boundaries "is a rough task but one with great rewards."[10] For example. my son observed our efforts to negotiate co-parenting, gaining resilience and conflict-resolution skills along the way. Studies show that positive co-parenting leads to better social adjustment in children, while hostility can breed withdrawal.[11] And as Dr. Michael Kerr observes, the differences between parents can spark "vigorous exchanges" that, when handled constructively, help children learn valuable lessons from healthy dialogue.[12] For our family, these exchanges—though sometimes tense—became opportunities to grow closer.

Humility and Redefining Identity

Andrew Murray wrote that humility is "the sense of entire nothingness that comes when we see how truly God is everything."[13] It is the act of surrendering to God his place and giving him the honor and glory he is due. "Humility always seeks, like Jesus, to be the servant, the helper, and the comforter of others."[14] In the context of a blended family, humility is key to unity. The voluntary choice to value others and maintain a modest view of oneself is truly beautiful and fruitful.

The paradox of the third Beatitude is that those who are "humbled" (in Greek, *praeis*, which can also be translated as "meek") experience a sweetness found in no other way. As Pinckaers notes, "true meekness is…the outcome of a long struggle against the disordered violence of our feelings, failings, and fears. In such instances, meekness implies tremendous inner strength..."[15]

As I watched my son prepare to marry and seek to build a reconstituted family of his own, I saw how humility has redefined our family's identity. In blended families, where roles shift and emotions run high, humility is a gentle resilience. It complements the patience, grace, and intentional communication Chapman and Deal describe (more on that in a minute), dismantling ego-driven barriers.[16] A stepparent who humbly acknowledges their limited initial influence—rather than demanding instant authority— invites trust, reshaping their identity from an outsider to a collaborative partner. When Jim humbly avoided demanding authority, choosing instead to earn my son's trust through quiet consistency, he became a true ally. Similarly, a child who humbly accepts a stepsibling's presence, despite loyalty conflicts, can move from a stance of rivalry to one of shared belonging. These approaches help loosen rigid family boundaries. They also break the cycle of resentment or entitlement, often carried over from past family dynamics.[17] When our children opened their hearts to one another, they took an active role in building the future of our family. Humility allowed us to co-create a new identity, not as fractured pieces, but as a unified whole.

Humility isn't weakness—it's the strength to lay down our assumptions, our need to control, and our expectations of how things should be, just as Christ did when he humbled himself to the cross (Philippians 2:8). Identities often feel unsettled, and roles are constantly shifting in our family dynamics, so humility becomes essential. It's what enables us to stop clinging to the old definitions of ourselves—or of others—and to receive a new name, a new place, from God.

For children like my son, who was deeply hurt by my marital struggles and felt displaced by changing roles, humility offers a path to restoration. When he lost his place as "the oldest," he likely had questions, consciously or subconsciously, such as, *Who am I now? Do I still matter? Where do I belong in this new family?* As his mother, I wanted to fix it, to restore what was lost. But God called me to humility—to listen, to walk with him prayerfully and faithfully through his journey of healing, to accept I didn't have all the answers, and to admit my role in his pain.

Through that season, I came to believe in Jesus as my Lord and Savior, and a few years later, my son did as well—and God reshaped us both. My son came to realize that his worth didn't hinge on where he stood in the sibling order, but on the unshakable love of his heavenly Father. And I learned that humility was what I needed to experience the rebirth I longed for. In Jesus, our identity is eternally secure as beloved children of God,* defined by his grace, and not by shifting roles or circumstances in our blended family.

Matthew 5:5 is an invitation to a transformation—from dysfunction, confusion, and pain to healing, identity, and belonging. "Blessed are the humble," Jesus says, "for they will inherit the earth." That's not just poetic—it's profoundly practical. Humility makes space for restoration. It allows us to release what's been taken from us and open our hands to what God longs to give. We all carry stories that long to be redeemed. But it takes humility to surrender our stories to Jesus Only then can we be redefined—not by our past or our roles, but by the grace that tells us who we truly are: loved, chosen, and never displaced in the family of God.

Turning Challenges Into Strengths

Our family has experienced all the stages of the developmental arc of a family blending proposed by Dr. Patricia Papernow, here condensed as: "fantasy" (initial optimism), "immersion" (facing reality), and "resolution"

---

* See John 1:12-13, Romans 8:14-17, 2 Corinthians 5:17, Galatians 3:26-28, Ephesians 2:8-10, 1 John 3:1

(settling into a new normal).[18] The journey was challenging for all of us, but with therapy, many tears, prayers, and countless honest conversations, we found a place of unity.

To guide us through this process, we turned to the practical wisdom of experts such as Gary Chapman and Ron L. Deal, whose insights in *Building Love Together in Blended Families* proved invaluable. They highlight three essentials that guided us: patience to let bonds form slowly, grace to forgive missteps, and intentional communication to break cycles of silence.[19] These three practices turned our challenges into strengths, shaping us into a family that's more empathetic and connected. They also taught our children skills they now carry into their own families: negotiation, conflict resolution, and the ability to navigate awkward conversations with love.

Humility is required to put each of these three essentials into practice.

Patience, the first essential, is critical in blended families, where emotional bonds don't form instantly. Unlike members of biological families with years of shared history, merged family members often need time to process feelings like resentment or insecurity. Patience allows space for differentiation (per Bowen), helping individuals manage their emotions without being overwhelmed by the family's collective tension. Patience requires humbly giving up our earnest desire for everything to be solved quickly, as it requires us to put the developmental needs of others first. With patient acceptance, family members can build emotional resilience over time.

Grace, offering favor and understanding, helps smooth the friction of ambiguous or shifting roles. In blended families, missteps are common: a stepparent might over-discipline, or a child might reject a new sibling or bark back at the stepfather, "You're not my dad!" Jim and I chose grace over frustration, sitting with our children to listen to their feelings without judgment. Again, this is a humble posture, and giving this grace can be hard! But grace prevents relational rigidity and resentment. This forgiving stance can redefine roles organically, allowing a stepparent to transition from "outsider" to "ally" without forcing authority, thus shaping a more adaptable family identity.[20]

And finally, as Chapman and Deal advocate, intentional communication disrupts negative patterns carried over from previous family experiences. Giving up our familiar patterns and assumptions takes humility. Yet, when family members intentionally talk about sensitive topics—such as a parent's previous divorce or a child's deep connection to a noncustodial parent—they begin to reshape long-standing patterns of conflict or silence. This echoes Kerr and Bowen's insight that interrupting generational cycles can lead to a stronger emotional foundation, shaping how family members relate to one another and future generations.

I'll never forget the candid conversation with my stepdaughter soon after Jim and I decided to marry. She's the kind of person who speaks her truth plainly. Her direct questions cut through the air, and I could sense the weight of her fears and disappointments about our new family dynamic. Though we'd known each other for years, my new role as her future stepmother stirred uncertainty in her about my intentions and sincerity.

As she spoke, I silently prayed for humility, patience, and grace to listen deeply and respond with an open heart, free from defensiveness. That moment of vulnerability and honesty laid the foundation for the strong and trusting relationship we cherish today. It taught me that embracing tough conversations with love and authenticity can forge bonds that endure.

When family members witness patience and grace in action—say during a mediated discussion about household rules—they learn constructive ways to navigate disagreements. Children absorb the skills of negotiation, conflict resolution, and navigating awkward conversations, carrying them into their social interactions.

Chapman and Deal's excellent book for families, which builds upon Chapman's book *The 5 Love Languages*, underscores that blended families don't just inherit dynamics, they actively build and nurture them through active love. Their insights suggest that while blended families face amplified challenges, these practices can turn complexity into a strength, shaping more empathetic, flexible, and communicative individuals. The dynamics of blending a family—parenting dilemmas, difficult ex-spouses, and children's expectations—are stressful but not beyond the capacity of a loving marriage to overcome with the help of Jesus. His humility is the foundational posture we must emulate. Nothing forms relationships better than genuine humility. While it demands tremendous psychological strength, humility has the power to reduce aggression within a family and foster lasting bonds of friendship.[21]

Nothing Is Wasted

Chances are that in your own family, you carry the weight of disruption—schedules, roles, loyalties, griefs, and the invisible tension of navigating it all. It can be easy to wonder, *Can anything beautiful come out of this mess?* But Scripture promises, and my family's story confirms, that God wastes nothing—not our tears, not our missteps, not even the confusing middle of the story. He uses it all to weave healing and hope. Even what feels broken beyond repair can become the very place where blessing begins to bloom.

I saw this firsthand in my son's journey. After going through a parent's divorce twice, losing his place as "the oldest," and wrestling through his questions of identity, he stepped into a new kind of leadership—not born out of position, but out of character. He became a connector in our family, consistently bringing humor into tense moments and noticing when someone needed encouragement. He never reclaimed the title of "oldest," but he earned something richer: the quiet respect of his siblings and the confidence that comes from knowing who you are, even when the family picture changes. That growth culminated as we gathered in our backyard, making his wedding a picture of redemption. His biological father, two stepfathers, six half-siblings, and their families celebrated together—a testament to God's unfailing love working beneath the surface all along.

If your family feels stuck in the in-between, take heart. The struggle may not vanish, but seeds are being planted. Trust God's timing, lean into humility, and hold fast to the promise that Jesus is weaving something beautiful. You may not see the fruit today, but in due time, it will bloom— more radiant than you could have imagined. Like trees rooted through storm and drought, we grow slowly, almost invisibly—and one day, we will look up and see that something beautiful has taken root. Still, even though humility, as we've already seen, opens the door to this transformation, it's only the beginning. In the next chapters, we'll explore how God's redemption takes these humble beginnings and builds a legacy of grace, healing the deepest wounds and planting roots that will sustain generations to come.

PRACTICAL TOOLS:

- **Self-Reflection Exercise**: Draw a diagram of your family, noting each member's role (e.g., peacemaker, caretaker) and unspoken expectations. Reflect: Where am I holding onto old roles that no longer fit? How can I align my role with God's truth about my identity?

- **Healing Discussion:** Gather your family for a low-pressure chat. Ask: "What role did you play in your original family, and how has it changed in our family?" Share how Scripture, like Matthew 5:5, has redefined your own identity through humility and grace.

- **Prayer Prompt:** Pray, "Lord, give me the humility to see my role clearly in our family. Heal each member where they feel displaced and show me how to support them with patience and grace. Let our family reflect your love."

- **Beatitudes Reflection:** Meditate on Matthew 5:5. Journal: What does "inheriting the earth" look like in my family? How can humility open doors to healing and hope in our daily interactions?

PART II.
God's Design and Faithfulness

CHAPTER 4

WHOLENESS

GOD'S ORIGINAL PLAN

Blessed are those who hunger
and thirst for righteousness,
for they will be filled.

—MATTHEW 5:6

Perhaps you know a family you might consider the "perfect" family. I think we all do. With admiration and, if we're honest, a hint of envy, we study them carefully. We stare at them in their coordinated outfits for their Christmas photo, watch their every move at church, or listen intently to each word they utter. We long to capture their secret sauce, to discover what makes their children behave respectfully, and what enables them to function with such peace and unity. Secretly, we want this family to succeed and to show us the way. And yet, when we hear the news of their impending divorce, we're not surprised. We know they are fallible people, just like the rest of us. There is a familiar ring to their strained relationship, secret battles, and the deep wounds they caused one another. Most of us have seen the picture-perfect family fall apart—and perhaps that family was our own.

For me, it was my uncle and his wife. They were devout Christians, attended church regularly, and served in their community. There are so many good aspects of my life that I can directly attribute to the way their relationship functioned. Anytime we visited their home, they were all smiles. I felt happy at their home, even though I couldn't name exactly what made me so. Today, this is something I care a lot about: making people feel happy when they visit our home. In fact, my aunt had an upright piano, and she allowed me to play it despite my lack of musical talent and training. To my husband's chagrin, I love playing instruments with my grandchildren. We create something that sounds more like joyful noise than music. My uncle and cousins worked around the house with a cheerful team spirit, and my aunt kept the kitchen sink clean of dishes even before sitting down to enjoy the meal. If you ever stay at our home for a meal, you'll notice two things: Jim and I work as a team, and I keep my kitchen sink spotless—to my aunt's credit. From my perspective, I was convinced they had mastered the art of maintaining a household, marriage, and parenting. When my mother told me that my uncle and aunt had filed for divorce, I remember the ache in my stomach and the words that escaped my lips before I could stop them: "Oh no...not them." I was very sad but also, strangely, not surprised.

Divorce rates among Christian couples are higher than we'd like to admit, though they fluctuate based on their religious commitment. According to recent studies, actively practicing Christians, such as those who regularly attend church, experience lower divorce rates compared to the general population.[1] Factors such as shared faith, community support, and covenant commitment foster stronger marriages among devout Christians. However, this does not mean that the possibility of divorce is eliminated. And while the divorce rate for blended families is hard to calculate, research shows that second marriages—Christian or not—have an increased chance of unraveling. It has been found that commonly quoted statistics were not based on any actual data, but some say the divorce rate for second marriages is as high as 50 percent and higher for blended families.[2] While no two blended families walk the same journey, some deal with many barriers and challenges. Every family has its struggles, and blended families start their journey together with more.

My heart was unsettled at the news of my uncle and aunt's marriage unraveling. If even *they* couldn't hold it together, what hope was there for families like mine—imperfect, barely patched together with threads of past heartaches, combined with our complicated histories and not-so-hidden resentments? It's like running a race but being forced to begin many miles behind the start line. Had we missed our opportunity to become the kind of family God blesses?

Are Blended Families Still Part of God's Design, and Can They Reflect God's Righteousness?

It's natural for us to crave love, connection, and peace in our family. But deeper still is our need for righteousness, for our homes to be built on what is just, right, and true. We should not be ashamed of this longing, as it reflects God's design. We were made to long for God's righteousness because it makes us whole, repairs what is broken, and creates the conditions for peace to exist. Peace and righteousness are partners in God's redemptive plan, and blended families are part of it.

Righteousness in Scripture isn't about maintaining appearances or avoiding failure by following the rules; it involves living in alignment with what is good, just, and holy—even when it's hard and costly. The Greek word we translate as righteousness is *dikaiosynē*. This important and complex biblical term can also be translated as justice, virtue, uprightness, or fairness. In the Old Testament, the Hebrew word for righteousness is *sedeq*, which carries similar meanings—what is right, what is honest, what is correct—and can even denote loyalty and salvation. Righteousness has legal, moral, and social aspects.

Despite the various translations, the theological significance of these terms lies in their reference to God's inherent righteousness and justice, not our own. Scripture teaches that righteousness is "imputed" or assigned to us through faith in Jesus Christ (1 John 2:1–2). Our salvation from the consequence of sin, our right standing with our Creator, is not something we earn or work hard to achieve (Romans 3:10); it is a gift of grace (Ephesians 2:8). Jesus, the Lord of lords, is our righteousness (Jeremiah 23:6). Righteousness is truly worth hungering after—and according to Jesus, more than we hunger for food. He said,

> So don't worry, saying, "What will we eat?" or "What will we drink?" or "What will we wear?" For the Gentiles eagerly seek all these things, and your heavenly Father knows that you need them. But seek first the kingdom of God and his righteousness, and all these things will be provided for you. Therefore, don't worry about tomorrow, because tomorrow will worry about itself. Each day has enough trouble of its own. (Matthew 6:31–35)

We don't have to make this hunger up; we all have a profound longing in our hearts for wholeness—what the Hebrew Scriptures call *shalom*. *Shalom* is more than peace and tranquility. It's the state where nothing is missing, and nothing is broken. Without righteousness (honesty, integrity, and justice), any peace we find is superficial or, at best, temporary. No righteousness, no shalom.

Scripture reveals that God created family, as seen in the story of Adam and Eve in Genesis 2:15–25, and families were created to display God's gifts of righteousness and peace. Family mirrors the unity, mutual care, and love that is found in the Trinity.* While our families may never fully embody that ideal unity, especially when shaped by complex histories and broken relationships, we are still invited to pursue it with intention.

Family flourishing arises not from flawless appearances but from "rhythms of presence, formation, and grace."[3] It is covenant love—steadfast, sacrificial commitment—that is the foundation of enduring relationships, not fleeting emotion or convenience.[4] When we root our homes in these truths, we embark on the slow, beautiful journey toward wholeness—toward not perfect families, but faithful ones.

Blended families may not resemble God's original design for family, but they are woven into God's redemptive story. While they carry unique scars and strengths, they, too, can reflect God's heart and unity. We're not the Trinity; we're human, and humans fracture. But God works through those fractures to make something surprisingly beautiful.

Blended Doesn't Have to Be Smooth to Be Beautiful

The idea of a "perfectly blended" family is a myth. No stepfamily becomes a seamless mix, and that's okay. The goal isn't fusion but healthy integration, where each member is valued and connected. Ron Deal, a leading voice on stepfamilies, emphasizes that these families thrive not by erasing differences but by embracing them with patience and grace.[5] In *The Smart Stepfamily Marriage*, Deal and co-author Dr. David Olson note that strong stepfamilies build on intentional communication and realistic expectations.[6] Healing and wholeness take time—sometimes years—and God is patient, faithful, and present in that slow becoming.

Over the past twenty years, our family has experienced a level of healing that often catches Jim and me by surprise. While we've had our ample share

---

* See John 17:21–23.

of conflicts, hurt feelings, frustrations, and disappointments, we have also grown to genuinely like each other and want God's best for each other. Our adult children, in-laws, and grandchildren have built relationships across bloodlines and are not reliant on our mediation for their unity or conflict resolution. Most have a relationship with Jesus and are pursuing godliness. As we all grow in Christ, our family dynamics reflect more of his grace, generosity, and sacrificial love. This is something I am convinced we could not accomplish on our own. I am reminded of this often, especially when we find ourselves in very uncomfortable conversations or conflicts.

Old wounds resurface, or hidden resentments rise from the depths, and once again, we're not as united as we'd like to be or thought we were. I used to lose hope when these would occur, until my dear friend, Jan, reminded me of how far we have come, "You're not back to square one, Inés. You may have gone back a few steps, but you're still making progress from when you started as a family." She's right. I keep her words hidden in my heart. As we work on reconciling yet again, it's a reminder that we're not perfect, but we're all pointed in the same direction: toward Jesus.

God doesn't expect your family to be perfect. He blesses the hunger for what is good, right, and just—even if it's messy. As Deal writes, "Success in a stepfamily is not about arriving at a destination; it's about journeying well together."[7]

Covenant Love and the Power of Redemption

One of the most powerful stories of redemption in a fractured family comes from Joseph in the book of Genesis. Born into a home with children from multiple mothers competing for attention and filled with favoritism, jealousy, rivalry, and betrayal, Joseph experienced the worst of a family gone wrong. He experienced injustice. Talk about not being perfect! His own brothers sold him into slavery, and his family was anything but whole. Yet, through years of pain and unexpected turns in his life, God brought healing not only to Joseph but to his entire household as well. In Genesis 50:20, Joseph told his brothers, "You planned evil against me; God planned it for good...." Joseph didn't deny the pain; in fact, "he wept so loudly that the Egyptians heard it, and also Pharaoh's household heard it" (Genesis 45:2), but he trusted God to redeem it. He hungered for God's righteousness. His story reminds us that no family is too far gone for God's restoring hand.

God's covenant love—his steadfast, unfailing commitment—forms the bedrock of families that continue seeking him, regardless of the circumstances. Michael Card describes the powerful biblical Hebrew word for this love, *hesed*, as "a love that will not let us go," a love that pursues us despite our failures.[8] This is the love God offers, and it's the love he calls us to embody in our homes. Jesus entered our brokenness to redeem it—not just in theory, but in real, messy lives, including our households.[9] Blended families, with their complex dynamics, are no exception.

Dietrich Bonhoeffer provides a compelling perspective on this; he wrote, "Christian community is not an ideal we have to realize, but rather a reality created by God in Christ in which we may participate."[10] In a merged household, this shared life—characterized by forgiveness, prayer, and mutual care—serves as a testimony of God's grace. Blended families uniquely demonstrate what only God can do: take the broken and make it beautiful again.

Jesus Redefined Family—and That's Good News for Us

Jesus turned the cultural view of family upside down. When informed that his mother and brothers were waiting for him, Jesus replied, "Whoever does the will of my Father in Heaven is my brother and sister and mother" (Matthew 12:50). For Jesus, the eternal family isn't defined by biology but by obedience to God and love for one another. This perspective was radical in a society where blood ties were everything.[11] It's still radical today.

One of Jesus' final acts on the cross was a moment of family-making. He looked at his mother and beloved disciple and said, "Woman, here is your son," and to the disciple, "Here is your mother" (John 19:26–27). Even in his last breath, Jesus wove new bonds of love—not through bloodlines, but through shared faith and commitment. Similarly, many blended families are formed not just by law, but by love. In Christ, we are given the permission—and power—to redefine what family can look like.

This is liberating news! Jesus created a space for spiritual kinship and for new definitions of belonging and loyalty. Stepparents, stepsiblings, and extended relatives can form bonds rooted in shared faith and commitment. Jesus made room for us—and now invites us to extend the same kindness to one another.

Righteousness Is About Pursuit, Not Perfection

In Matthew 5:6, Jesus declares flourishing for those who "hunger and thirst for righteousness." Righteousness isn't simply rigid moral perfection; it's alignment with God's heart—his justice, mercy, and love. To hunger for righteousness in family life means pursuing God's way, even when it's difficult, by choosing forgiveness over resentment, patience over frustration, and grace over judgment. In doing so, the promise is striking: *they will be filled*. Not with ease or accolades, but with God's presence, peace, and power.

In Scripture, righteousness is often connected to right relationships—with God *and* with people. It represents relational wholeness, not personal perfection. When we pursue righteousness in our homes, we lean into God's heart for reconciliation. This entails owning our part, forgiving offenses, and creating space for new beginnings. Hungering for righteousness may manifest as engaging in a difficult conversation, choosing humility over defensiveness, or simply remaining at the table when everything in you wants to walk away. It's through these quiet acts of faithfulness that God fills us—not with immediate results, but with enduring hope.

The hunger is the qualifier. If your family yearns for God's righteousness, you are already set apart for his blessing. Every prayer whispered over a tense dinner table, each effort to listen to a stepchild's heart, and every choice to love despite past hurts—these are acts of righteousness that God acknowledges and honors.

Maybe you're reading this and thinking, "This all sounds great, but my situation is different. My family is a disaster. We've messed up too much. The damage is done." If that's you, take heart. The Beatitudes weren't written for the already blessed—they were spoken to the broken, the burdened, and those barely holding it together. Hungering for righteousness doesn't require a clean record; it simply requires an open heart. God specializes in starting over. And when we bring him our mess, he doesn't flinch—he gets to work. Don't underestimate what God can do with a family that is willing to seek him again and again. He is faithful to restore and renew.

Your Family Can Be a Living Testimony

Redemption isn't merely something God does *for* us—it's also something he does *through* us. As blended families pursue righteousness, they become living reflections of God's restoring work. Your family—yes, *your* family— can embody the beauty of the gospel. It won't look like a Christmas card with coordinated outfits. Instead, it may resemble tearful reconciliations, hard-won trust, or quiet moments of laughter after years of strain. But it's real, and it's holy.

You are blessed to bring about good. Your hunger for righteousness, however imperfect, however out of reach righteousness might feel, is an invitation for God to work wonders in your home. Keep pursuing him. You will be filled. May the words of the psalmist encourage you: "Light dawns for the righteous, gladness for the upright in heart. Be glad in the Lord, you righteous ones, and give thanks to his holy name" (Psalm 97:11–12).

Pursuing righteousness isn't just a concept to believe in—it's a practice to live out. We will always hunger and thirst for justice in this world—and therefore within our families.[12] Whether our family feels fractured or thriving, we must cultivate God's presence and wholeness in our home. I hope the practical tools at the end of this chapter can provide you with some ideas on how to maintain this posture. However, as we move on to the next chapter, we'll see there is something we must do to progress on the journey of becoming: invite God's transformative power into our homes to disrupt the patterns of dysfunction and cycles of hurt. A different future is available to us, but we must be willing to embrace something thoroughly countercultural.

.

PRACTICAL TOOLS:

- **Self-Reflection Exercise:** Where do you see signs of God's design (his righteousness and justice) at work in your family? In what areas of your life are you finding it difficult to embody that vision? Write down one to two areas you want to bring before God this week.

- **Healing Discussion:** Daily Family Blessing: Practice speaking one word of affirmation to each family member daily. Celebrate kindness, courage, and small acts of service. Build a rhythm of declaring God's blessing over each other.

- **Prayer Prompt:** "Lord, make our family hungry for your righteousness. Fill our home with your love and grace. Teach us to love beyond biology, to forgive quickly, and to walk in step with your Spirit."

- **Beatitudes Reflection:** Meditate on Matthew 5:6 as a family. What does it mean to hunger for righteousness together? Identify one step you can take this week to lean into that hunger (e.g., extending forgiveness, praying together, honoring a hard conversation).

CHAPTER 5

BREAK-THROUGH

BREAKING CYCLES OF HURT AND DYSFUNCTION

Blessed are the merciful,
for they will be shown mercy.

—MATTHEW 5:7

It was a fleeting moment—a sharp word, a familiar tone, a passing glance that carried more weight than intended. In that split second, I was no longer in the present. I became a child again, standing in the shadow of old wounds; I became a spouse caught in the echo of a past relationship's pain. At that time, I had been married to Jim for two years, my third marriage, and this particular argument made me wonder if I'd made another mistake—all because of a simple kitchen mat!

My mother loved gifting me modern conveniences, like the thick drying mat she gave me for hand-washed dishes. I loved it and told my family, kindly but firmly, that although the mat was by the sink, this was no excuse for them to leave dishes on it—it was meant to be part of the routine: wash, dry, and put away. Weeks later, I noticed that dishes were consistently left on the mat. Each dish left on the mat felt like a dismissal of my efforts, echoing the invisibility I'd felt as a child cooking for a household of eight while my cousins played. Frustrated, I finally hid the mat and told Jim I had thrown it away. I expressed very emotionally that I felt the dishes had been left for me to put away, which made me resentful. As I type this, it seems like a minor issue, but this exchange erupted into a massive argument between Jim and me. It escalated to the point where we retreated to different parts of the house to cool off—angrily, Jim went to the couch, and I went to the upstairs bathroom in tears.

I didn't know it then, but our argument wasn't just about a drying mat. It represented a history of pain for both of us.

For me, the pain of feeling unseen, unappreciated, and abandoned started when I was a little girl. Nothing I did was ever good enough for my mother's critical eye. My father's absence since I was an infant left me without manly, loving arms where I could be comforted, encouraged, and seen. A wound of past injustices awoke in me every time I walked by the kitchen and noticed the dishes left on the mat, long after they had dried. No one thanked me or saw my effort when I put them away.

For Jim, my outburst echoed his father's disproportionate and explosive anger. When Jim was in his early teens, the family was preparing to attend a funeral. Jim's father noticed that the debris from tree trimming had not been picked up as he had ordered and expected. To this day, Jim recounts this story with an emotional tone, recalling how his father kicked him so hard in the behind that he believed his tailbone was broken. He remembers the frightening feeling of being a skinny teenage boy being chased by a two-hundred-pound man with an anger that seemed excessive for the situation. Not long after that day, Jim watched his father drive off with his luggage in the family car, leaving Jim to announce the shocking news of the divorce to his mother. The wound never left.

Dishes left drying on the counter are no big deal to Jim, and a wife taking care of household chores is what his mother modeled. Thus, my reaction felt disproportionate, and once again, he experienced the pain of having a loved one turn on him, together with the ensuing fear of an unprovoked attack. To me, however, it was a symbol of neglect. Despite our years of knowing each other before we married, I knew nothing about his tender heart, injured by his father's explosive anger, and he knew little about my drive for perfectionism fueled by a hypercritical mother and a fatherless upbringing.

In that emotional exchange, we triggered each other's deepest wounds, unaware. The moment passed, but its impact lingered, a stark reminder that the past doesn't suddenly vanish. It persists, weaving into our present until someone dares to break the cycle. Our story isn't unique. All of our families often carry unseen wounds that surface in everyday moments, threatening to repeat the cycles we hoped to leave behind.

The Cycles We Unwittingly Repeat

While we might like to believe we are better than the families we came from, every so often a painful moment challenges our illusion. An explosive argument unfolds with an eerie familiarity. A spouse slams his fist against the wall in anger. You feel yourself emotionally shutting down in response to a sarcastic comment. Suddenly, it feels as though the past horrors are happening again. With their intricate tapestries of histories, hopes, and hurts, blended families are particularly vulnerable to these cycles.

The patterns of conflict, dysfunction, or emotional distance we faced in childhood or previous relationships do not simply vanish when we enter a new family. They follow us, often masquerading as default reactions—passive aggression, snapping at a stepchild, withdrawing from tense moments, or clinging to control to avoid vulnerability. These responses may feel familiar, even natural, but they often stem from unhealed wounds from past relationships. Even when we vow to do better, to leave those ways behind, we instinctively default to what's familiar, much to our horror. Left unaddressed, these patterns become the blueprint for our family's future, repeating the same struggles we longed to escape. They threaten the health of our marriage and family dynamics. They threaten our ability to show compassion toward one another and the harmony we long to build.

The first time my son married, just before the ceremony was to start, he gathered privately with his two half-sisters. In a solemn pinky swear, the three of them vowed to break the family legacy of divorce, pledging to start a new lineage of enduring marriages. Divorce was not an option. They were so young and hopeful, and in hindsight, unprepared for the weight of that promise. After all, we cannot control the actions of our spouses. Within a decade of marriage, two of them faced the heartbreak of divorce, each with two children. The pain of those broken vows cut deeply, leaving scars of disappointment and doubt for all of us. My youngest daughter, the only one without a reconstituted family, confided her fear of succumbing to the same cycle, even though she was not struggling in her marriage. I, too, wrestled with a sense of powerlessness, watching the shadow of divorce loom over our family once more.

Recognizing the Cycle

Breaking these cycles begins with seeing them clearly. Then, we must choose to change them, as far as they are within our control. Our default reactions that arise under stress and fatigue (contempt, anger, withdrawal, fear, or perfectionism) are valuable clues to past wounds hidden in our hearts. Our intense responses become red flags, indicating an opportunity for exploration, healing, and growth. We often assume that our emotional reactions are solely about the current event, but a deeper history underlies the present.

Yet, there is hope. In Christ, our past does not have to define our future. Jesus, who absorbed the penalty for our sins and offered mercy on the cross,* shows us how to absorb pain without perpetuating it, empowering us to rewrite our family's story. The gospel offers a radical invitation: to break the cycles of hurt and dysfunction through self-awareness, intentional change, and the transformative power of God's mercy. This may be why the fifth Beatitude turns our attention from our attitude to our actions. We are called to emulate God's heart of charity: "He has not dealt with us as our sins deserve or repaid us according to our iniquities" (Psalm 103:10).

The Weight of Unseen Patterns

Blended families are beautiful mosaics of second chances—often rebuilding from broken pieces—but they also carry the weight of multiple pasts. A stepparent may unknowingly mirror the criticism they received as a child, while a stepchild might retreat into silence, echoing the isolation they felt in a previous family dynamic. These patterns are often intergenerational, passed down like an unwritten script. This legacy can manifest as criticism, silence, or control, thus perpetuating disconnection unless we intervene.

Consider Sarah, a stepmother who learned to cope with her parents' arguments by staying silent and invisible. Now, when tension arises

---

* See Romans 6:23; 8:1; 1 Peter 1:3; 3:18; 1 John 2:2.

between her husband and his teenage daughter, Sarah freezes and retreats emotionally. Her silence, once a survival mechanism, now creates distance in her new family. Her stepdaughter interprets it as rejection, and the cycle of misunderstanding grows.

Sarah's story is not unique. Most of us carry baggage; however, it can become for us "good baggage," as Ike Miller calls it in his book *Good Baggage*. Miller proposes that past wounds, when examined, can cultivate resilience and wisdom.[1] But first, we must recognize them for what they are.

The next time you react strongly, snap at your spouse, shut down during a disagreement, or feel an overwhelming need to "fix" a situation, try this: pause and journal. Ask yourself: *When have I felt this before? What does this feeling remind me of?* These questions, inspired by John Bradshaw's *Homecoming*, help us uncover the wounded inner child or past experiences driving our behavior.[2] Awareness alone doesn't heal, but it illuminates the path forward.

The Power of Mercy to Break Our Old Cycles

In the Scriptures, mercy emerges as a profound theme that reflects God's character and inspires his work of salvation. Paul summarizes it in Ephesians 2:3–5:

> We were by nature children under wrath...God, who is rich in mercy, because of his great love that he had for us, made us alive with Christ even though we were dead in trespasses. You are saved by grace!

When we extend mercy to others through forgiveness and aid, it not only reflects God's mercy but also invites God's mercy toward us. This fosters a different cycle, taking us from the cycle of pain to a cycle of grace that transforms relationships. Pinckaers contends that "true mercy transcends pity and 'kind feelings.' It is rooted in the depths of our wills, at the level of charity and the virtue of justice."[3]

Mercy, as depicted in Scripture, carries two interconnected yet distinct meanings that together form a powerful call to action. First, mercy means not receiving the punishment we deserve—offering compassionate forgiveness or leniency instead of deserved discipline. Forgiveness might seem like a sign of weakness compared to the power of revenge, but it is not. Showing mercy demands tremendous strength, as it involves conquering our inner urge to demand the justice we believe we are owed. Second, mercy encompasses charity and loving-kindness toward those in need, actively meeting the struggles of others with compassion, grace, and support, even when unearned. These facets weave together like threads in a tapestry, creating a fuller picture of mercy as both a restraint from causing harm and proactive goodness.

This does not imply excusing harmful behavior, remaining in danger, or tolerating abuse. If you face physical, emotional, or psychological harm—especially in abusive systems—mercy toward yourself and others requires seeking immediate help from professionals, authorities, or support networks to establish safety and boundaries. Mercy is wise and protective, and never enables ongoing harm; it disrupts cycles of pain without perpetuating them.

Every day, we have opportunities to practice mercy from the heart, but we must first receive it to give it freely. Jesus embodied mercy. On the cross, he offered forgiveness to the undeserving, and in his ministry, he healed the sick and fed the hungry. In Matthew 5:7, he declared that those who extend mercy will receive it, and he taught in Luke 6:35–36, "Love your enemies, do what is good, and lend, expecting nothing in return. Then your reward will be great, and you will be children of the

Most High. For he is gracious to the ungrateful and evil. Be merciful, just as your Father also is merciful."

I want to emphasize this very important point: *Mercy is not passive. It is an active disruptor of cycles of pain.* It is extended not to the perfect or the polished but to the merciful. We must become givers of what we most long to receive, starting by accepting God's mercy. The gift of mercy we receive through Jesus is the mercy we can, then, pass on. As Paul urges in Romans 12:17, "Do not repay anyone evil for evil. Give careful thought to do what is honorable in everyone's eyes." Blended families, especially due to their complex history, have opportunities to actively recognize unhealthy cycles of hurt and dysfunction, take practical steps toward healing, and embrace mercy as the cornerstone of transformation. Like a revitalizing river from God's boundless loving-kindness, mercy results in our flourishing.

When Jim and I exploded at each other about drying dishes, I ran to the furthest room in the house from where he sat. The upstairs bathroom seemed remote enough for me to feel safe to cry out to God. In a pool of tears and with a heart full of fear, I asked God a slew of questions: Would this third marriage also fail? Would my daughters have to suffer a second divorce and my son a third? Was there any hope for a woman like me to ever find someone to love? Did I even know how to love? Like Job when he was peppering God with his complaints, I first heard nothing in response. Then, I had the surprising courage to ask God a bigger question: Can you teach me how to love Jim the way that you love me? The answer came quickly—and I didn't like it. *Mercy.*

It had to be the Holy Spirit speaking to my spirit because I could not have come up with this idea on my own. He prompted me to go downstairs and tell Jim, "I am sorry." "Oh no," I exclaimed out loud, "why would I do that?! He was the one...blah, blah, blah." Then I sensed God interrupting me with this question that popped into my mind, "Did you just ask me to teach you to love the way I love?" Embarrassed at how quickly I forgot my request, I decided to follow the prompt. Then, another prompting came as I sensed the Holy Spirit giving me instructions, not audibly, but in my mind, "When you go downstairs, get on your knees and put one hand on his knee, then say what I told you to say." This was way more than I could handle. With my Puerto Rican passion flaring, I feared my upset might jolt us and overwhelm us both. But I wiped my tears and started what felt like the *Green Mile** walk to the living room downstairs.

As I walked to our living room, my feet felt glued to the floor, much like the dinosaurs must have felt when they got stuck at the La Brea Tar Pits† in Los Angeles, thousands of years ago. It took every ounce of will-power to move one foot in front of the other and keep myself from turning around. When I arrived at the entrance to the living room, Jim was sitting on the couch, his eyes betraying his anxiety about what I was about to say or do. In silence, I approached him, knelt, and placed my right hand on his left knee. Slowly, the words came out: "I am sorry." That is all I said, and we just stayed like that for who knows how long. The heavens must have rejoiced, for a stubborn sinner chose to trust God and act in the ways of Jesus. That day, I decided not only to apologize—which I did honestly—but also, feeling that I was hurt by Jim, too, I chose to offer mercy, to give up my "right" to punish him or make him pay for what he did or said (forgiveness), and to extend kindness by humbling myself to meet his emotional need in that moment (charity). I absorbed the pain and gave it to Jesus to help me heal. And a miracle happened!

---

* The *Green Mile* refers to the final walk taken by a death row inmate from their prison cell to the execution chamber. The term comes from Stephen King's novel *The Green Mile* (New York: Scribner, 1996), in which a death row at Cold Mountain Penitentiary has a floor made of green linoleum—thus, prisoners walk the *Green Mile* on their way to execution. The phrase has since been used metaphorically to describe any final journey toward an unavoidable fate, often with somber or spiritual undertones. It's a somber journey toward surrender.
† To learn about the La Brea Tar Pits, visit https://tarpits.org/.

To this day, Jim and I believe that moment changed our marriage forever. This was over twenty years ago, but we both remember it as if it were yesterday. We learned to trust Jesus with our marriage and follow his example: to trust, love, and show mercy his way—wisely blending forgiveness with active compassion, day by day.

The Action of Mercy

Mercy is not weakness, nor does it imply tolerating abuse. It is a strength rooted in the gospel. You can forgive without subjecting yourself to harm by setting boundaries to protect your well-being while still reflecting God's grace. For example, forgiving a stepchild's hurtful comment might mean understanding their fear while calmly addressing the behavior. Just as God extends unmerited grace to us, we are called to extend it to others. He calls us to "be merciful, just as your Father also is merciful" (Luke 6:36). This might involve offering compassion to your spouse when they revert to old habits, recognizing their efforts to grow. Or it could mean showing yourself mercy when you stumble, trusting that God's grace is sufficient for your journey. Ephesians 4:32 urges, "Be kind and compassionate to one another, forgiving one another, just as God also forgave you in Christ." Mercy reflects this call, transforming our families through grace.

Consider the story of David and his stepdaughter, Mia. Mia's biological father had been emotionally distant, and she struggled to trust David's affection. She resented David's appropriate actions to maintain order and discipline in the home. When Mia rejected his attempts to connect and snapped, "You're not my dad," David felt hurt and withdrew. But after praying to Jesus, asking for his help and wisdom, David chose a different path. Instead of retreating, he wrote Mia a note: "I'm here for you, no matter what, and I know this is hard." His mercy—expressed through self-control, patience, and understanding—opened the door to trust. Over time, Mia began to see David not as a threat, but as a father figure—a person who was eager to support and care for her lovingly. Mercy rewrote their story.

Mercy is the gift we receive and the gift we give, and in that exchange, healing takes root.

In blended families, mercy is a game-changer. It softens the edges of conflict, fosters forgiveness, and creates a safe space for growth. When we offer mercy to a stepchild who lashes out, a spouse who misunderstands, or even to ourselves when we fall short, we disrupt the cycle of pain and invite transformation. Yet, the offering of mercy requires wisdom: knowing when it means forgiving and when it means providing tangible support to someone who is struggling, all while guarding against enabling poor behavior.

Intentional Change: Rewriting the Script

Healing is not automatic. It requires intentional steps to disrupt old patterns and establish new ones. You cannot heal what you're not willing to name. This means creating a family culture rooted in grace, communication, and mutual respect. And make no mistake, communication is key! A blended family without healthy communication will struggle deeply. In their work *Healing What's Hidden*, Evan and Jenny Owens outline practical steps for spiritual and emotional healing, emphasizing the importance of confronting pain head-on.[4] This might mean seeking counseling to process past trauma, practicing new communication habits, or setting boundaries to protect your family's emotional health.

Intentional change begins with small, consistent choices. For example, if you grew up in a home where conflict was avoided, you might commit to addressing issues openly with your spouse or stepchildren. If criticism was a constant in your past, you might practice affirming your family members daily, even in small ways. These choices, though uncomfortable at first, rewrite your family's relational script. They signal to your family and yourself that the past no longer holds the pen.

One powerful tool for intentional change is self-reflection. The *Breaking Patterns Journal* exercise detailed at the end of this chapter guides you to name patterns you want to change, reflect on past struggles, and commit to new actions that foster a legacy of growth. For instance, if you have avoided discussing your stepchild's resentment to keep the peace, commit to one honest conversation a week, starting with, "I've noticed you seem upset—can we talk about it?" This small step builds trust and disrupts avoidance.

A Blessed Future

The past may have shaped you, but it does not define you. In Christ, you have the power to break cycles of hurt and dysfunction, replacing them with a legacy of love and redemption. This means you have a unique chance to showcase God's grace, building a future where faith and resilience can shine brightly.

This journey isn't without setbacks or moments when old patterns resurface. But each act of mercy, prayer, and reflection moves you closer to a family rooted in love. Breaking cycles is not just about stopping pain but about building something new. Your flourishing family's legacy begins with practical steps like engaging in healing discussions that foster vulnerability and celebrate progress, while reinforcing your shared commitment to a healthier future. Another powerful practice is prayer, which anchors your family in God's redemptive power, reminding you that He is the ultimate cycle-breaker.

As I said in the introduction, and it's worth repeating here: while all families can reflect God's redemption, healthy blended families have a unique opportunity to spotlight its beauty. Love, resilience, and faith can define your family's future. Transformation unfolds as a journey. Recognize that individuals may be at different stages along the path, and that's okay. Each intentional choice is an offering that God can use for your flourishing. In Christ, you are not bound by the past. You are blessed to rewrite the story, forging a family built on redemption rather than repetition.

Your family can become a testament to God's grace through awareness, intentional change, and the transformative power of mercy. As you receive mercy from God and extend it to others, you create a home where healing takes root and hope flourishes. Blessed are the merciful, for they will be shown mercy.

The following tools empower you to take steps toward breaking cycles and building a new legacy. Try one or all to start your journey of transformation. As you approach mercy, your family's new story begins now.

PRACTICAL TOOLS:

- **Self-Reflection Exercise:** Breaking Patterns Journal: Write down a specific pattern you've noticed in your family—perhaps a tendency toward defensiveness or emotional withdrawal. Next, describe its impact: how does it affect your relationships? Finally, write a commitment statement outlining one new action you'll take to break this cycle. For example, *I commit to pausing and praying before responding to my stepson's frustration, choosing empathy over defensiveness.*

- **Healing Discussion**: Gather your family and invite each member to share one thing they want to change (e.g., "I want to stop yelling when I'm stressed") and one way they've seen growth (e.g., "I've been more patient this month"). Encourage honesty and support, foster vulnerability, and celebrate progress.

- **Prayer Prompt**: Dedicate an evening to intercede for your family's growth. Pray for wisdom to recognize unhealthy cycles, strength to build new patterns, and hearts open to mercy. Invite each family member to contribute a prayer or Scripture, creating a sense of unity and purpose.

- **Beatitudes Reflection**: Set aside time to meditate on Matthew 5:7 and ask: *Who in my family needs mercy right now? How can I extend it?* Then, reflect on how receiving mercy from God empowers you to be a cycle-breaker. Write down one specific way you'll show mercy this week—perhaps by listening without judgment or apologizing for a past mistake. After acting on it, journal how it felt to extend mercy and how God's grace sustained you.

CHAPTER 6

REDEMPTION

EMOTIONAL AND SPIRITUAL HEALTH

Blessed are the pure in heart,
for they will see God.

—MATTHEW 5:8

I visited my mother on a Tuesday, as was my usual routine, but I found her visibly sad and disappointed. Without my prompting, she shared that she was becoming acutely aware that her sewing skills were failing. All day, she had been working hard to finish a set of quilted coasters, and her many mistakes were discouraging. I have never attempted quilting, and my response must have proven my lack of experience. Turning her gaze away from me, she hopelessly whispered, "You don't understand." Her response stung my heart because I had tried to comfort her. The mostly completed quilted coaster she held in her aging hands was beautiful and excellently constructed. Sure, some of the stitching seemed a little wobbly, and the coaster wasn't perfectly shaped into a square, but the elaborate pattern was impressive. Although I struggled to admit it, she was right: I did not understand.

Creating a quilt is a meticulous art form. It requires patience to piece together diverse scraps of fabric layers and stitch them into a harmonious whole. It's difficult to balance colors, patterns, and textures while ensuring structural integrity. Quilting demands both technical skills as well as a creative vision. My mother knew what she was trying to create, and the result did not match her vision. And, since I could not get into her headspace, nor for that matter, her heart, I could not possibly understand how hard this was for her.

Similarly, blending a family involves weaving together unique personalities, histories, traditions, and much more. No family's process of integration is identical because no two families are alike. It is an art form—an intentional expression of human creativity, imagination, and emotion; and it has the potential to become a beautiful creation. Each family has a sense of what may be possible if they could achieve health and a resilient bond. This is why we may feel discouraged when our vision for a healthy family does not match the reality we are a part of.

But take heart: there is a way to remain committed to the blending effort while holding the hoped-for results more loosely: by seeking to see God at work in our imperfect family.

Seeing God at Work

In the Bible, seeing God is associated with intimacy, favor, and transformation. Moses longed to see God's glory (Exodus 33), David sought to gaze upon the beauty of the Lord (Psalm 27:4), and Jesus revealed the Father to us in human form (John 1:18). In the new creation, we are promised the joy of seeing God face-to-face (Revelation 22:4). For the "pure in heart," this dual blessing offers the promise of both spiritual communion today and eternal fulfillment tomorrow.* Yet this vision begins in the present when we submit ourselves to God's transformative power.

---

* It echoes the priestly blessing in Numbers 6:24–26, which invokes God's face shining upon his people, symbolizing favor and closeness.

Hebrews 12:14 reminds us that holiness is necessary, for "without it no one will see the Lord." When individuals within the family seek emotional and spiritual health—when they lay down bitterness, jealousy, and shame—they are seeking purity of heart, and they begin to see God more clearly in their story. They witness his fingerprints on their healing and align their desires with God's desires. They recognize his voice in moments of reconciliation. Each other's act of Christlike grace is yet another opportunity to see God at work.

I offer encouragement, practical tools, and biblical wisdom in this book, but I recognize that your family differs significantly from mine. Even a fellow traveler on the blended family road may be just as blind to your personal struggles and disappointments as I was to my mother's battle with quilting. Still, I know this is true: God is presently at work in your family. In fact, the psalmist declares this truth:

God is our refuge and strength, a helper who is always found in times of trouble. (Psalm 46:1)

There are many Hebrew words to describe the God of the Bible. Each name was revealed to God's people in specific contexts and described different aspects of his faithfulness, power, provision, or presence. Just as a quilter selects patterns to create something meaningful, the many names of God reveal the richness of who he is to us in every season. The Hebrew word for God used by the psalmist in Psalm 46:1 is *Elohim*, meaning the "supreme God." We are not speaking of any deity, but rather the Creator of all things who is sovereign over Heaven and Earth, eternal, and unmatched in power and glory. The apostle Paul wrote that Jesus is "the image of the invisible God" (Colossians 1:15), and Matthew declares he is God with us, "Immanuel" (Matthew 1:23). Jesus is the artist working to mend your hearts and transform your family into a beautiful creation.

Believe me when I say nobody cares for you as much as Jesus does, and nobody is more willing to sacrifice for you and your family. The question is, do you see him, or are you seeking to see him?

Let me say it again so it sinks in if it hasn't already: Jesus is at work in the blending of your family, piece by piece.

The Art of Blending

Since Jesus is actively at work in each of his followers—and in our families—he makes healthy blending possible and hopeful. Emotional health and spiritual health are foundational for thriving.

According to the American Psychological Association, emotional health can be defined as the ability to manage one's emotions in productive and healthy ways. Mental health, says the APA, is "a state of mind characterized by emotional well-being, good behavior adjustment, relative freedom from anxiety and disabling symptoms, and a capacity to establish constructive relationships and cope with the ordinary demands and stresses of life."[1] Emotional healing is possible through many means, but Jesus offers us what no secular source can—the healing of the soul.

Spiritual health is the state of being deeply connected to God, grounded in his truth, and guided by the Holy Spirit. In spiritual health, our lives are marked by trust in His love, alignment with His will, and a growing capacity to love others with grace and humility as Jesus loves us.

However, a more powerful and life-changing effect occurs when we integrate our emotional health with our spiritual health. According to Peter Scazzero, "Together they offer nothing short of a spiritual revolution, transforming the hidden places beneath the surface...people's lives are dramatically transformed."[2] Scazzero contends, "Emotional health and spiritual maturity are inseparable."[3] Without spiritual grounding, emotional healing becomes superficial. Without emotional honesty, spiritual growth stalls.

Emotional and spiritual health enables the weaving together of love, trust, and unity, so its members can flourish amid complexity. These elements do not emerge accidentally or easily; they are cultivated with intention, much like a quilter carefully selects the colors and pieces of fabric and determines their placement in the finished whole. To experience emotional health, we must be willing to identify, name, and heal the wounds from past losses, betrayals, or transitions. We must invite God's grace into our wounds, allowing him to transform pain into peace, resentment into reconciliation, and confusion into clarity. Resources like Peter Scazzero's *Emotionally Healthy Spirituality* can guide this journey.[4]

Faith is a powerful balm. In the words of Brené Brown, "Connection is why we're here; it is what gives purpose and meaning to our lives."[5] Faith amplifies this connection, creating a spiritual thread that binds the family together and makes God's presence palpable. Surrendering emotional wounds to Christ fosters reconciliation and peace. As you build through your faith in Jesus, your family's emotional healing "quilt" will look uniquely yours. Yet, all families that trust Jesus to bring healing have this in common: God's transformative fingerprint.

As we pursue spiritual health and healthy relationships within our families, God will purify our hearts, and we will be able to perceive that transformative fingerprint more and more clearly.

The Healing Work of Grace, Piece by Piece

Jesus' words in Matthew 5:8 offer us hope for our journey of blending: "Blessed are the pure in heart, for they will see God."

Perhaps you don't like the verse, as these days the word *pure* is often used as a polite stand-in for *sheltered,* or maybe you grew up in some version of Christian legalistic purity culture, which left you wounded. At first glance, Jesus' words may seem an impossible, unattainable standard. How could we ever experience the flourishing promised in this Beatitude, especially as a blended family?

The New Testament often describes a heart wholly devoted to God as "pure."* The Greek word for "pure," *katharos*, refers to something clean, untainted, and free from corruption—whether physically, morally, or spiritually. James 1:27 connects *katharos* with compassionate action and a lifestyle untouched by worldly corruption. Paul emphasizes that true love flows from a pure (*katharos*) heart, from inner purity and integrity (1 Timothy 1:5). The pure heart is free from duplicity, hypocrisy, or corruption.

Indeed, none of us can cultivate a pure heart on our own. It lies outside the reach of our mere willpower.[6]

Scripture reminds us that we "all have sinned and fall short of the glory of God" (Romans 3:23). So, the point is not to try harder to make yourself pure and holy, but to seek the pure One by faith. It is by grace that we have been saved, through faith in the life, death, burial, and resurrection of our Lord Jesus Christ. As Paul reminds us in Ephesians 2:8–9, "You are saved by grace through faith, and this is not from yourselves; it is God's gift—not from works, so that no one can boast." Yet, as Pinckaers notes, "purity remains a central and characteristic virtue of the Christian life."[7]

This is why we must rely on Jesus to bring purifying healing to our hearts and to our families.

Matthew 5:8 speaks to a heart refined by God's love—not perfect, but open to transformation. When Jesus preached this, he was referring to

---

* See, for example, Matthew 5:8, James 1:27, 1 Timothy 1:5, and 2 Timothy 2:22.

the Hebrew understanding of your heart as the center of your being, your mind, and emotions, making this verse applicable to any area of your life. As King David prayed in Psalm 51:10, we, too, can cry out, "God, create a clean heart for me." He penned these words after committing adultery, arranging for an innocent man's murder, and hiding all of it under his kingly authority.* Biblically, to be pure in heart is not to be flawless but to be open, honest, and surrendered.

This, we can do! And the promise attached to this Beatitude is extraordinary. The pure in heart will "see God"—not just in eternity but here and now, in glimpses of his grace, presence, and power.

This promise becomes an anchor for families that have undergone reconstitution. In seasons of struggle, the invitation to pursue purity of heart reminds us to bring our whole selves—mess and all—before God. It invites families to cultivate emotional honesty and spiritual dependence. And it promises a divine reward: the ability to perceive God at work even through the chaos. We may not be able to change, deny, or defy our circumstances, but we can be content amidst them, surrendering our family into God's loving arms.

My mom and I spent some time talking about her quilted coasters and the many other quilted items she had constructed over the years. Looking around her apartment, I could see some of them: the tablecloth, the quilt decorating her wall, and the bedspread. They were all beautiful. However, these coasters are still special to me. They were crafted by her aging, trembling hands—the last items she made before Alzheimer's disease stole her mental acuity. The beautiful, multicolored coasters symbolize her determination and ability to create beauty, even if imperfectly. I still use the coasters today. My mom taught me that it's never too late to create beauty, but we must set aside our drive for perfection, comparison, and denial.

---

* Read the story of David's great sin and repentance in 2 Samuel 11–12, Psalm 32, and Psalm 51.

As the author of Ecclesiastes reminds us, there is a season for everything under the sun, but the time for trusting in God never ends.*

Pursuing Emotional and Spiritual Reconciliation

Like a quilter stitching torn fabrics, God weaves reconciliation into fractured families. One of Scripture's most powerful stories of emotional healing and reconciliation is that of Jacob and Esau. The twin brothers carried decades of unresolved pain and were torn apart by deception. Yet, Jacob's spiritual transformation gave him the courage to pursue reconciliation. He took tangible steps—sending gifts to his brother, approaching him in humility, and trusting God with the outcome (Genesis 33). Esau, in turn, chose forgiveness. He embraced his brother, restoring what was lost. Their story holds an important lesson for us: healing begins with God. Our emotional wounds do not have to define our future. With God, even fractured families can be made whole.

While the following are composite stories, they reflect experiences I have witnessed in real families I've met as a pastor. The Bennett family, a newly merged household, faced constant tension. Lisa's daughter Sophie resented her new stepbrother Ethan, and Ethan carried deep wounds from his mom's absence. Their relationships slowly softened through nightly prayers and spiritual rituals like gratitude jars. Sophie began to voice her pain honestly as faith in Jesus became the foundation for the family. Ethan found empathy in his stepmother's prayers. The family grew closer through the practice of gratitude. Emotional health took root when spiritual practices created space for God to work.

Navigating cultural and religious differences, the Nguyen family began hosting monthly "family faith nights." When stepsiblings Linh and

---

* Ecclesiastes 3:1–8; 12:13.

Caleb collaborated on a song, it marked a turning point. Their spiritual connection bridged emotional distance. Like Jacob and Esau, they took practical steps to move from rivalry to respect.

Jacob's path to reconciliation began with a profound spiritual experience. As he wrestled with God, he was transformed, receiving a new name (Israel) and a new perspective (Genesis 32). This encounter empowered him to face his brother with humility and courage. Similarly, faith can be a catalyst for healing in disconnected families. By surrendering their hurts and fears to God, family members can gain the strength to forgive, empathize, and rebuild trust. Though it may take time and persistence, faith practices like prayer, confession, and worship anchor families in God's grace. I have seen this at work in my *Smoothie* family.

Building Trust and Unity

The promise of seeing God offers a profound source of hope for navigating the complexities of our unique family dynamics. In the presence of emotional challenges—such as past hurts, jealousy, or feelings of disconnection—this promise serves as a beacon of healing and unity. It reminds us that our journey is part of a larger story of redemption, where God's grace can mend broken relationships and restore peace. It also encourages us to embrace vulnerability, extend forgiveness, and lean into our weaknesses, knowing that God's strength is perfected in our efforts to cultivate purity of heart. This eternal perspective shifts our focus from daily trials to the ultimate blessing of divine intimacy, fostering a sense of purpose and communal support. This hope is not just a distant reality but a present assurance that our pursuit of emotional and spiritual health will be rewarded with the transformative presence of God.

Still, finding trust and unity is like making a quilt: it requires patience and the willingness to begin anew. Jacob and Esau only embraced after years of estrangement (Genesis 33:4). Yet their reconciliation is a poignant symbol of restored trust and unity. Trust is built through consistent, loving actions over time. As Chris Voss observes, "The most dangerous negotiation is the one you don't know you're in."[8] Many families live with emotional undercurrents they haven't yet named, such as bitterness from past relationships, jealousy between siblings, fear of being replaced, and insecurity in a parent's love. Healing begins by surfacing these realities and naming them with honesty and compassion. Voss's empathetic listening techniques—such as mirroring emotions and validating feelings—are helpful here, and using them can turn tense exchanges into opportunities for understanding.

Building on Chapter 5's exploration of mercy, we see that empathetic listening opens the door to forgiveness, which is the foundation for healing. Esau's forgiveness of Jacob is a testament to the transformative power of letting go of past grievances. Despite the pain Jacob had caused, Esau chose to embrace his brother rather than hold onto resentment (Genesis 33:4). Forgiveness is often the key to unlocking emotional and spiritual health. It's not about forgetting the past but about choosing to release its hold on the present. As Scazzero writes, "Forgiveness is the only way to break the grip of the past."[9] Trust and unity forged through listening and forgiveness are an ongoing pursuit, not a finish line.

Overcoming Common Challenges

Every blended family will encounter challenges, but emotional and spiritual health offers a way through. Jacob's fear of Esau's reaction mirrors the anxiety that we might feel when addressing past hurts or navigating sensitive issues. However, just as Jacob found that his fears were unfounded when Esau welcomed him warmly, we often discover that open communication and vulnerability can lead to unexpected breakthroughs.

For example, children may feel torn between their parents, yet open, affirming, and respectful conversations, like a phone call with a child's biological parent, can help dissolve guilt. Disagreements on discipline can sow confusion, but when parents work at setting unified expectations, they bring clarity and calm to their home. Your children's need to mourn the changes they are experiencing and the loss they have endured may result in behavioral issues, yet honoring what they miss and creating a safe environment to share their memories and struggles opens their hearts to what is new. Each of these challenges offers an opportunity for the Holy Spirit to purify the heart—to remove fear, pride, or bitterness, and replace them with love, grace, and truth.

As flawed humans, we wrestle with imperfections, yet the hope of Matthew 5:8, "Blessed are the pure in heart, for they will see God," reminds us that God is refining us daily. The Holy Spirit, as Romans 8:26 assures us, "helps us in our weakness," guiding us toward purity even when we stumble. Offering ourselves grace begins with self-compassion: acknowledging our struggles, seeking forgiveness, and trusting God's patience. Likewise, we extend grace to others by recognizing they, too, are works in progress, deserving of kindness despite their flaws. Patience grows as we lean on the promise in Philippians 1:6—"He who started a good work in you will carry it on to completion"—and choose to love through challenges, knowing we're all being shaped by God's hands.

A pure heart, as described in Matthew 5:8, isn't about being perfect or immune to pain; it's about being open to God's love and direction, even in tough situations. When we seek purity in Christ, he will help us lead with the fruit of the Spirit: love, joy, peace, patience, kindness, goodness, faithfulness, gentleness, and self-control (Galatians 5:22–23). The Holy Spirit will help us practice empathy, establish boundaries without resentment, pray persistently, and seek community support.

It's natural to feel hurt or discouraged when family members don't join you in this surrendered posture toward Jesus. However, having a pure heart doesn't depend on their choices—it rests in your commitment to love as Christ does, trusting God to sustain you, and aligning your desires with his. Your faithfulness can be a quiet light in their lives, even if they don't recognize it yet. Keep relying on God's strength, and you won't just cope— you'll grow through it. As you focus on being faithful to Jesus, your surrendered heart becomes a window through which they, too, might see God.

Just as a quilter weaves together diverse fabrics with care and intention, blended families can stitch their unique stories into a quilt of love. Your family quilt becomes a testament to God's redemptive power and blessing. Each prayer, each act of forgiveness, adds a stitch to a legacy of healing, reflecting the beauty of a heart surrendered to Christ—a legacy that will shine for generations.

PRACTICAL TOOLS:

- **Self-Reflection Exercise:** Dedicate fifteen minutes weekly to self-reflection. Journal about emotions like resentment or insecurity affecting family ties. Pinpoint specific triggers—perhaps a stepchild's defiance or a spouse's past—and pray for clarity. Assess where bitterness, resentment, or insecurity might be affecting family relationships. Write down any areas where you feel resistance to forgiveness and unity.

- **Healing Discussion:** Develop a weekly plan for family devotions. Start with a ten-minute weekly devotion. Read a short Scripture (e.g., Matthew 5:8), discuss its meaning, pray together, and end with affirmations.

- **Prayer Prompt:** Use targeted prayers to address specific needs. For example: "Lord, reveal my hidden hurts and give me grace to love where it's hard." Ask God to reveal any areas where healing is needed. Pray for the strength to extend grace and patience in your family.

- **Beatitudes Reflection:** Reflect on Matthew 5:8 and consider what having a "pure heart" means in your family relationships.

PART III.
Pathways to Flourishing

CHAPTER 7

KINDNESS

NAVIGATING CO-PARENTING AND STEPPARENTING

Blessed are the peacemakers,
for they will be called sons of God.

—MATTHEW 5:9

We all have a heart's desire for a family brimming with love, joy, and unity. Most of us are willing to work for it. Yet, as blended families, we often feel far from achieving this vision of flourishing. The path is often tangled with conflict, distrust, and differing histories. Just as a fragile seedling cannot thrive unless nurtured diligently with water, sunlight, and care, a family requires deliberate effort to flourish. We're all prone to view our families through either a romantic or a pessimistic lens. Our mindset needs the occasional reset. Here it comes—not from me, but from Jesus.

In the Sermon on the Mount, Jesus calls his disciples to a radical pursuit of peace—not a superficial truce, but a commitment to reconciliation and unity with grace and intentionality. This pivotal Beatitude in Matthew 5:9, "Blessed are the peacemakers, for they will be called sons of God," is especially important for our households. We've explored how forgiveness lays the foundation for healing, and how being open to God's purifying work in our hearts equips us to build upon that foundation, layering deeper emotional and spiritual wholeness. Now, we turn to peacemaking, a deliberate pursuit that fosters unity within our families. Its payoff is that we will reflect God's redemptive love.

The Greek term *eirēnopoioi* ("peacemakers") denotes that peacemaking doesn't involve distorting what is true, avoiding conflict, or forcing harmony. It literally means, "makers of peace"—an "endeavor to reconcile persons who have disagreements"[1] through a deep and intentional commitment to love, understanding, and wisdom, despite challenges. Jesus' call emphasizes not just living at peace but also actively pursuing peace. This aligns with the Hebrew concept of *shalom*, a holistic well-being that encompasses justice, harmony, and wholeness. To achieve this peace, we must establish trust and confidence. Researchers like Dr. James Bray remind us that trust in our families is not automatic; it is built over time through consistent, intentional acts of love.[2] Pursuing peace is slow, steady work.

Peacemaking is as vital to a blended family as sunlight is to a plant.

We are all called to work for peace and pursue reconciliation with spouses, neighbors, and all people—insofar as the matter is up to us (Romans 12:18). Amid tension, often at personal cost, being a peacemaker reflects God's redemptive purposes through Christ (2 Corinthians 5:18–19). Hence, this Beatitude's blessing aptly promises that peacemakers will be called "sons of God."* As his beloved children, we will look like our heavenly Daddy, our "Abba" Father (Romans 8:14–16).

For stepparents and co-parents, navigating relationships with stepchildren, ex-spouses, and in-laws makes the sacred calling of peacemaking both a privilege and a challenge. Some relationships grow over time, while

---

* In Matthew 4:9, the term *uioi theoū* translated by the Christian Standard Bible as "sons of God" denotes both men and women, heirs of the Kingdom. In the Old Testament, Israel has the title "sons" (Deuteronomy 14:1; Hosea 1:10). See also Romans 9:26.

others may remain strained or distant. Still, we're called to pursue peace, trusting that God sees our efforts and will bring healing in his way and in his time. While day-to-day dynamics may not always be easy, they provide opportunities to reflect God's heart. Peacemaking is not about achieving unhindered harmony. Thankfully! This would be an impossibility for us humans. But it does reflect God's grace in our daily struggles. We can lean on the Holy Spirit to help us cultivate unity and reconciliation and extend grace to ourselves and others. We are all works in progress.

One more point, which I will state in the words of Pinckaers: "Those who have an inner love for peace are certainly most likely to spread peace around them; even to fight for it. The peaceful person is not necessarily a mild, timid creature who cannot take a stand."[3] This inner strength for peace prepares us to take bold steps toward reconciliation, as I learned in a pivotal moment with my stepdaughter.

The Olive Wreath: A Symbol of Peace

The aroma of coffee and fresh pastries created a comfortable setting for a tense conversation. My stepdaughter chose this small café for our "white-knuckle conversation," the term she used to capture our mix of anxiousness and intentionality. The café hummed with the clink of cups and the murmur of conversations, but my stepdaughter and I sat in our own little world. On the table lay an olive wreath I'd crafted from a neighbor's branch that morning. The olive branch is considered a symbol of peace due to its biblical association with the dove returning to Noah's ark, signaling the end of the flood and God's reconciliation with humanity.* In ancient cultures, it also represented prosperity and harmony, and was often extended as a gesture of goodwill.[4] With this in mind, I offered the small wreath as

---

* See Genesis 8.

a symbol of my desire for peace and wholeness between us. It became a witness to our dialogue about her most pressing question: Do you love me?

How does a stepmother prove her love?

I recalled a lesson learned from *Never Split the Difference* by Chris Voss, which likens high-stakes conversations to hostage negotiations where something precious is at stake. Voss writes, "The goal is to identify what your counterpart actually needs (monetarily, emotionally, or otherwise) and get them feeling safe enough to talk and talk and talk some more about what they want."[5] For us, the "hostage" wasn't the details of our disagreement but the love and trust in our relationship. Though this wasn't a hostage negotiation, the stakes were high. We'd had several meetings before this one, but they did not end well. As we spoke that day at the café, my nervous fidgeting softened, and my fears of failing her, of widening the gap, eased.

We sat for a few hours, sharing our thoughts, listening, and sometimes pausing in silence to hold hands and shed tears. We explained our perspectives on our relationship, revealed our heartaches, and discussed the most recent issue that had fractured our unity. I asked probing questions, seeking clarity about her most pressing desires, and none of them were unreasonable or beyond my capacity to fulfill. The coffee grew cold, yet our hearts warmed as both of us felt heard and loved. The problem that brought us to this moment seemed less significant; however, we talked about it and came to believe that we could agree to disagree and still love one another. What mattered most was to build our relationship in a way that was founded on trust and transparency so it could have the resilience to handle the occasional conflicts. After setting a few goals to stay connected, affirming our commitment to each other, and praying, we left the café in unity, convinced that God had led our conversation with his divine wisdom and grace.

We've talked about plants as a metaphor in this chapter, and I can't help but notice that the olive branch, that symbol of peace, comes from a plant that takes years and years to come to maturity. Our family relationships are, like an olive orchard, something that must be cultivated over *years* if they are to come to full maturity and fruitfulness. The Psalms depict the household of the happy as one where the children are "like young olive trees around your table" (Psalm 128:3). The olive tree is also used in Scripture as a symbol of peace, not only in our relationships with other people, but with God himself. "But I am like a flourishing olive tree in the house of God," David rejoices in Psalm 52:8, "I trust in God's faithful love forever and ever."

At that meeting with my stepdaughter, I realized that proving love in a blended family is less about words and more about the slow, steady work of showing up, listening, and pursuing peace—no matter how long it takes.

When words won't do, commit to being present.

The Unwelcome Enemy That Never Rests

Our café conversation showed me that peacemaking requires more than human effort. It demands spiritual strength. We said that peacemaking is to families like sunshine is to plants. But there are almost-invisible enemies that can attack plants: diseases. fungi, and tiny insects. Beyond our struggles, an unseen enemy seeks to unravel the love we build. We're not just dealing with differences or conflicts between people—our skirmishes can carry spiritual weight. Two imperfect women, not yet fully perfected by Jesus, with sinful natures and personal wounds sat at that café table. Paul writes about the believers' ongoing tension of sanctification, specifically in Romans 7:18–19. The two of us had to ask the

Holy Spirit to take our thoughts captive to obey him. We relied on him to help us manage our selfish tendencies, triggers from wounds, temptations, and coping mechanisms. But, as Christians, we were aware that believers also experience spiritual warfare.

The apostle Paul writes that "our struggle is not against flesh and blood" but against spiritual forces (Ephesians 6:12) who seek to unravel all that is good and belongs to God. Satan targets God's creation and his people with unceasing malice (1 Peter 5:8). Through deception and division, he sows discord in relationships, twisting bonds of love and trust into strife and isolation. He perverts hearts by tempting believers to stray from God's truth, exploiting vulnerabilities like trauma and sin to lead our minds astray from devotion to Christ, as he did with Eve (2 Corinthians 11:3). Yet, God's grace empowers his people to resist and stand firm against the enemy. To return to our plant metaphor, God is like an all-knowing gardener who understands exactly which weapons are needed to fight the disease attacking the plant. God shares his weapons and tools with us. Paul urges believers to "put on the full armor of God" to stand in victory (Ephesians 6:11). The devil is a thief, and he desires to "steal and kill and destroy" our relationships (John 10:10), but Jesus rescues us with his love.

Equipped with God's truth and our honest love for each other, my stepdaughter and I quickly communicate whenever we experience tension. I apply Paul's wisdom from Ephesians 4:26–27 to our family: "**Be angry and do not sin.** Don't let the sun go down on your anger, and don't give the devil an opportunity." With the help of Jesus, the Prince of Peace (Isaiah 9:6), no matter how daunting a conversation feels, peace, insight, and resolution lie beyond it. The tougher the discussion, the richer the joy of resolution that awaits. However, even then, trust is built slowly, day by day.

Earning Trust Through Love

Stepparenting is a delicate dance of patience and wisdom. Unlike biological parents, stepparents cannot assume authority or affection. They must earn respect through servant-hearted love, offered freely without expecting immediate reciprocation. This process can be challenging and move more slowly than we'd like. Respect doesn't grow in a straight-line; sometimes, we will go backward before going forward. Along the way, we're required to navigate the delicate balance of being a parent-like figure while respecting the child's loyalty to their biological parents. Trust is worth fighting for, though, because trust is a vital component of peace. When we trust someone, we don't feel the need to take up arms against them—neither to attack them nor to defend ourselves. In addition to delicately balancing our roles as a stepparent and co-parent on the road to trust, we'll also need abundant patience as tensions or disagreements are often mistaken for a lack of love or favoritism toward biological children, if they're present.

Erich Fromm, in *The Art of Loving*, reminds us that love is not a passive feeling but an active practice that demands concentration and insight.[6] Almost two thousand years earlier, the apostle Paul expressed this clearly in his letter to the Corinthian church, using not adjectives but *verbs* to describe love. Love is action: it *is* patient, kind, and enduring, never keeping score, rejoicing in truth; it bears, believes, hopes, and endures all things—and it never ends.[*]

For a stepparent, active love might mean listening to a stepchild's frustrations without taking them personally, offering support without demanding gratitude, or simply being present through years of awkward silences. Love is a marathon, not a sprint, and it flourishes when we commit to showing up, even when the results are not immediate.

---

[*] See 1 Corinthians 13:4–8a.

Likewise, co-parenting with an ex-spouse can feel like walking a tightrope. Conflict is inevitable, but as Dr. Jenna Flowers outlines in *Coparenting*, healthy co-parenting prioritizes the children's emotional and spiritual well-being above personal grievances. Advocating for a "conscious parenting" approach, Dr. Flowers states that "through empathetic understanding and tolerance, you create a safe environment where you truly hear your child's ideas and concerns."[7] This requires maturity, clear communication, and a commitment to working together rather than against each other. Peace is possible when co-parents choose to focus on what unites them—their love for their children—rather than what divides them.

Peacemaking doesn't erase disagreements but approaches them with humility, wisdom, and patience, like when we calmly discuss schedules or forgive someone for the sake of a child's stability. Matthew 5:9 reminds us that peacemakers are blessed not because they eliminate conflict but because they reflect God's heart.

Cultivating Unity: Grace and Intentionality

Unity in a family is not automatic—it must be cultivated with intentionality. This might involve creating new traditions, setting healthy boundaries, or making a conscious effort to invest in one-on-one time with each family member. I can't recommend this enough! But more importantly, it is achieved by modeling God's grace. In blended families, this is how we will achieve peace in our co-parenting and stepparenting roles.

Paul Tripp, in *Parenting*, calls parents to love their families in light of the grace and hope we have in Jesus. Grace, as the cornerstone of biblical parenting, allows us to extend forgiveness when tensions arise, and hope reminds us that God is at work, even in the messiest moments. He writes,

"God never calls you to a task without giving you what you need to do it. He never sends you without going with you."[8]

Again, this reminds me of the story of Joseph and his brothers in the book of Genesis. Their family was fractured, marked by jealousy, betrayal, and separation, yet ultimately held together through God's redemptive grace. Joseph's choice to extend forgiveness (Genesis 45:4–8) wasn't a single moment but a deliberate process. He had years to reflect on the injustice and trauma he experienced at the hands of his brothers when they sold him into slavery, but upon seeing them, he offered them grace. First, he "treated them like strangers and spoke harshly to them" but still sent one of the brothers with "grain to relieve the hunger" of their families (Genesis 42:7, 19). Having favor and authority given to him by Pharaoh, king of Egypt, Joseph could have easily retaliated by sending his brothers away to die of starvation or imprisoning all of them indefinitely. But, as you continue reading the story, you'll notice that Joseph's expression of grace grows ever so slowly, as he orders his workers to provide the brothers with extra grain, return their payments, and give them provisions for their journey. Eventually, Joseph breaks down in tears and draws near to his brothers, offering extravagant forgiveness. As we noted back in chapter 4, he "wept so loudly that the Egyptians heard it, and also Pharaoh's household heard it," and he "kissed each of his brothers as he wept" (Genesis 45:2, 15). Grace is receiving a gift that you do not deserve. It's costly.

In a blended family, grace operates similarly: it's not a one-time act but a daily posture, a willingness to see each family member not as a rival or outsider but as a thread essential to the family tapestry. This perspective shifts our question from "How do we fix this conflict?" to "How is God weaving us together through this moment?" Grace is a posture that invites patience, humility, and surrender to God's larger design.

Additionally, grace is lived out in daily moments. It's found in humble apologies, compassionate listening, and intentional acts of kindness. When I listened to my stepdaughter's grievances, I wasn't negotiating with her. I was seeking to extend the grace I received from Jesus by affirming her worth and mirroring the way God listens to me in my brokenness. Grace frees us from creating a family based on legalism; instead, we create a home where mistakes are met with mercy. In a blended family, this freedom is revolutionary. It dismantles the walls of "yours" and "mine," replacing them with a shared identity as God's children. The olive branch carried by the dove to Noah wasn't just a sign of dry land; it was a promise of God's presence, a pledge that he would never abandon his people. Grace is that olive branch. It is an assurance that God is present in the floodwaters of conflict and is sufficient to hold the family together.

Extending grace is how peacemakers nurture unity.

Unity also requires setting realistic expectations. Not every relationship will be harmonious—fully unified in love and purpose—and that's okay. Some stepchildren may take years to warm up, if they ever do; some ex-spouses may remain combative. Pursuing harmony doesn't mean tolerating toxic behavior. Healthy boundaries protect your family while allowing you to act with integrity, trusting God with the outcomes. Grace doesn't erase the differences; it sanctifies them. The unique struggles—navigating co-parenting schedules, blending traditions, or healing past wounds—are not obstacles to unity but the very materials God uses to create something beautiful. This perspective invites a radical trust so that every hard conversation, every moment of forgiveness, and every act of listening will contribute to a legacy of love that reflects that we are citizens of God's Kingdom, where diverse lives are woven into a harmonious whole.

When Peace Seems Elusive

While we strive for harmonious relationships, not every interaction in our family will be peaceful. This is a sad reality, but it is something we must learn to accept. Some individuals—whether an ex-spouse, stepchild, or in-law—may be determined to perpetuate conflict, no matter how much we seek calm. Romans 12:18 offers a sobering yet freeing reminder: "If possible, as far as it depends on you, live at peace with everyone." This verse acknowledges that a peaceful state is not always achievable, but it calls us to do our part with faithfulness and integrity, trusting God to work through and beyond our efforts.

Pursuing harmony and peace while protecting your family might mean limiting contact with a toxic co-parent, calmly enforcing boundaries with a defiant stepchild, or releasing unrealistic expectations. It's about trusting God with the unresolved tension and continuing to act with love, knowing that Jesus sees your efforts. Again, as Matthew 5:9 promises, peacemakers are blessed—not because they resolve every conflict, but because they reflect God's character in their pursuit of peace.

Blessed to Cultivate Peace

Peacemaking is a journey, not a destination. We cannot expect a complete absence of arguments, disagreements, and friction. My stepdaughter and I didn't resolve every tension that day at the café. But as we talked, laughed, and even cried, the olive wreath on the table reminded me of the peace I was called to pursue. Through flexibility and prioritizing love over control, it is possible. Peacemaking is not a one-time act but a daily choice to show up, extend grace, and trust God with the rest.

We must pursue a "noble peace," as Pinckaers describes, not a shallow peace born of fear, avoidance, or weariness. Such peace is cowardly, external, and built on concession or compromise, failing to foster true healing.[9] Noble peace, rooted in truth, justice, and generous love, flows from the heart and leads to flourishing, as we saw in Chapter 6's call to emotional and spiritual health. This type of peace flows from our hearts by the power of the Holy Spirit as a gift from the Lord of peace (2 Thessalonians 3:16, James 1:17). This peace aligns with God's redemptive work, transforming relationships through courage and commitment.

Some days, you'll hold an olive wreath of progress; others, you'll face storms of conflict. As you navigate the complexities of stepparenting, co-parenting, and building unity, remember that you are not alone. Jesus, the ultimate Peacemaker, walks beside you, weaving grace through every hard conversation and quiet act of love. He will offer wisdom and strength for the journey. Blessed are you for pursuing peace; you are building a home where God's Kingdom shines.

PRACTICAL TOOLS:

———————

- **Self-Reflection Exercise:** Family Covenant: Create a written agreement outlining family values, expectations, and relational commitments. If appropriate, include the children in the process. Craft a simple olive branch (real or symbolic, like a drawing or ribbon) with your family. Place it in a shared space as a reminder of your commitment to peace. When tensions arise, gather around it to pray or discuss things calmly, reaffirming your love.

- **Healing Discussion**: Identify and share ways you have built trust and connection with stepchildren and between each other (shared hobbies, one-on-one outings, etc.).

- **Prayer Prompt:** Ask God to give you wisdom and inspiration to take specific steps toward peace in your family—whether through controlling your tongue, direct conversation, acts of kindness, or simply choosing to extend grace.

- **Beatitudes Reflection:** Reflect on Matthew 5:9 and consider how Jesus promises that those who pursue peace reflect the heart of God. In seeking peace, you are building a home where love, respect, and God's presence can flourish. How does this encourage you?

CHAPTER 8

RESILIENCE

PARENTING AND DISCIPLESHIP

Blessed are those who are persecuted because of righteousness,
for the kingdom of heaven is theirs.
You are blessed when they insult you and persecute you
and falsely say every kind of evil against you because of me.
Be glad and rejoice, because your reward is great in heaven.
For that is how they persecuted the prophets who were before you.

—MATTHEW 5:10–12

We tend to think of discipleship as a program that the church runs through small group experiences and Sunday services—an effort reserved for elite Christians or those in professional ministry. But for Christ-followers, discipleship encompasses every believer and every area of life. It is not optional or something to engage in when one feels ready to commit. Discipleship is a process—a lifelong journey of following Jesus, learning his teachings, and emulating his character. The Holy Spirit does the work of transformation as we submit to God's will and purposes.

Jesus' Great Commission (Matthew 28:19–20) calls believers to make disciples, teaching others to obey his commands. Discipleship represents both a personal commitment and a familial responsibility, requiring intentionality to guide everyone toward faith amidst diverse backgrounds.

Forming a blended family with children from previous relationships or in-laws can be a great joy and is richly rewarding. It offers everyone in the family the opportunity to experience profound love, broaden their relationships, increase support, and gain exposure to different perspectives. However, children may feel uncertain about the new family dynamics, protective of their relationships with their biological parents, and worried about living with new stepsiblings. The family may struggle to coalesce around shared values when there is a lack of alignment among adults, extended family, and/or children in matters of faith. These are just a few of the many factors that can create unwanted conflict and discord. Nevertheless, every obstacle, especially the most distressing one, presents an opportunity to model Christlike love and resilience.

If you are a child of any age in a blended family reading this, know that your unique experiences and feelings matter deeply to God. He sees your uncertainties, loyalties, and hopes. He is inviting you into this discipleship journey right alongside your parents and siblings, if any. As you navigate these changes, remember that Jesus is your ultimate guide, turning every challenge into a chance for your faith to grow strong and your character to become Christlike. While I am speaking to parents below, I trust that you'll find the principles in this chapter still helpful to you.

The apostle Paul's words have become our mantra in enduring the myriad of changes and challenges we face as a family:

> Let us not get tired of doing good, for we will reap at the proper time if we don't give up. Therefore, as we have opportunity, let us work for the good of all, especially for those who belong to the household of faith. (Galatians 6:9–10)

To fully embrace our opportunities to love as Jesus loved us, we must commit to faithfulness and steadfast discipleship. Our consistency will instill biblical values in our children and grandchildren, while honoring their unique journeys. As we persevere, we not only nurture faith but also become living testimonies of God's grace. But let me be straightforward with you: it's going to be hard work.

How Hard Can It Get?

Although the Beatitudes in Matthew 5 are typically regarded as eight in number (verses 3–10), some interpretations count them as seven by potentially merging similar themes or drawing from source-critical hypotheses, whereas others extend the count to nine by including verses 11–12 as an additional blessing addressing direct persecution. I concur with Pennington that Matthew uses *markarioi* (blessed) nine times in succession, perhaps signaling nine Beatitudes. However, in this chapter, I combine the eighth and ninth *markarioi*, as the latter expands on the same theme.[1] The eighth Beatitude, as commonly understood, "Blessed are those who are persecuted because of righteousness, for the kingdom of heaven is theirs" (Matthew 5:10), speaks to the challenge of standing firm in faith amid opposition. Christians worldwide face severe persecution, ranging from social exclusion and imprisonment to physical harm. In the words of Christian martyr Dietrich Bonhoeffer, they suffer for the "sake of a righteous cause."[2]

I don't mean to diminish the terrible injustice and suffering that many of our brothers and sisters around the world have endured and continue to endure as they hold to their faith in Jesus. Our personal experience of persecution may not compare to theirs in terms of severity; however, we must not dismiss the relevance of this Beatitude to our lives and, consequently, to our journey as a family.

The words of the apostle Paul to his disciple Timothy serve as a sober reminder: "All who want to live a godly life in Christ Jesus will be persecuted" (2 Timothy 3:12). In case you missed it, he said *all*. Even though it will be on a different scale than those who suffer physical harm and death, those pursuing righteousness and Christlikeness in a blended family can invite resistance and rejection. For instance, an ex-spouse or extended family member may undermine our efforts to build a Christ-centered home, or a child may resist biblical teachings or sarcastically question our faith in light of our past experiences. We may be accused of being disingenuous or rejected for expressing our faith at family events.

My husband says that we've "been hit by softballs" when it comes to persecution, and I concur. But if a softball has ever hit you, you know, it still hurts. While it is not the same as experiencing severe hostility, being treated with skepticism, rejection, social judgment, and misunderstanding can sting and create pressure to conform. These tensions are not equivalent to extreme persecution, but they test our commitment to faithfulness and can tempt us to compromise our values.

Living in harmony with God's standards often puts believers at odds with the world. The Greek word *diōkō*, translated as "persecuted," refers to driving away, pursuing, or running after and harassing someone, especially because of beliefs.[3] Jesus prepared his disciples for such opposition, urging them to endure it with courage and view it as a blessing. Similarly, we should not be surprised by pushback from within or outside the family when pursuing righteousness (Matthew 5:6), integrity (v. 8), or peacemaking (v. 9). Again, if you're reading this as a child in a blended family, the pushback can come from your siblings or even your parents. Opposition may come as subtle criticism, social pressure, or relational strain from those unsettled by your allegiance to Christ.

As believers, we must also guard against becoming persecutors ourselves. It's easy, even with good intentions, to judge or pressure family members—parents, ex-spouses, children, stepchildren, or in-laws—who hold different beliefs or are at earlier stages of their faith journey. Instead of imposing expectations, we're called to show the mercy we learned in Chapter 5, offering patience and understanding to nurture their growth, not hinder it. We are called to foster environments where individuals feel safe to explore faith at their own pace, and in response to the prompting of the Holy Spirit.

Nevertheless, by leading with love, perseverance, and an unwavering commitment to biblical truth, we parents can cultivate a home where God's Kingdom shines. The reward lies in witnessing our loved ones grow in faith, embracing the reality that every family is a work in progress but can reflect God's grace and redemption. True discipleship is evident through lived examples, not just words.

Tested Faith

This Beatitude became real for me in a moment of honest questioning from our daughter, a reminder that even mild opposition tests our faith. Looking down at my brand-name shoes, our daughter said to me, "I need to know. Are you for real?" I knew what she was asking. This was my first pair of Tory Burch® shoes, which I could now afford to buy thanks to Jim's financial stability. She was interested in knowing if the posture of my heart reflected the faith I had recently professed. Concerned that the fancy shoes indicated my heart was plagued with greed compounded by impure motives for marrying her father, all the while I declared my trust in Jesus, she added, "Is your faith genuine?" It was a fair question. I was impressed by her courage in asking it, so I paused and then responded, "With time and suffering, we will know."

Scripture teaches that time reveals the fruit of faith or its absence. In Matthew 7:15–17, Jesus instructed the disciples to discern whether someone was a false prophet by examining the fruit of their words and actions. Using the illustration of trees bearing fruit, Jesus suggests that it takes time to discern because one must wait for fruit to grow to inspect its quality. Likewise, the Bible teaches that suffering tests the condition of our hearts and unveils our trust in God's promises. The apostle Peter reminds us that grief, through various trials, serves a greater purpose: it proves the character of our faith (1 Peter 1:6–7). When he refers to "various trials" (*poikílos peirasmós*), he is speaking of all manner of experiences. This phrase appears only one other time in Scripture: when James uses it in his admonition to "consider it a great joy" whenever we experience "various trials" in James 1:2–4. Christians, indeed, have suffered greatly for their faith. In Pinckaers' words, it is because Christians "proclaim the Gospel and wish to live it, and thus to follow their Master, that they are attacked, treated as liars, and manhandled."[4] Still, neither Jesus nor James speaks of joy *in* the suffering, but joy *after* the suffering.[5] That said, we must not go about searching for suffering or comparing our struggles with those of others; each of us has our own.

Speaking about this very point, Bonhoeffer wrote,

...so that no one presumes to seek out some cross or arbitrarily search for some suffering, Jesus says, they each have *their* own cross ready, assigned by God and measured to fit. They must all bear the suffering and rejection measured to them. Everyone gets a different amount. God honors some with great suffering and grants them the grace of martyrdom, while others are not tempted beyond their strength. But in every case, it is the one cross. It is laid on every Christian.[6]

Believers are called to persevere. Thus, Christ-centered blended families are as well, and they must trust that their efforts—even their suffering—to raise family members in faith will yield good fruit. When parents face resistance from exes, children, stepchildren, or external critics for upholding biblical principles, they can find comfort in being blessed by God. Jesus said,

> You are blessed when they insult you and persecute you and falsely say every kind of evil against you because of me. Be glad and rejoice, because your reward is great in heaven. For that is how they persecuted the prophets who were before you. (Matthew 5:11–12)

To be blessed signifies a deep spiritual joy that is independent of external circumstances. Jesus promises that enduring hardship for faith connects believers with God's Kingdom, both now and eternally. As believers, we "stand in a noble succession of true servants (i.e., the prophets) who endure opposition and hostility for the sake of God's redemptive plan."[7] However, our reward in Heaven exceeds our earthly accomplishments.

It has been over twenty years since our daughter asked me the question, "Is your faith genuine?" She now has much more information to form an opinion about the state of my faith. Still, since I am a saint in progress, my answer remains the same: Time and suffering will tell.

Every Christ-following parent is a saint in progress[*]—called holy by God because of Jesus' righteousness imputed upon us, yet growing through the daily walk of discipleship. If you are a parent facing mild opposition, like a child's resistance to prayer or a friend's skeptical

---

[*] See, for example, Romans 1:7, where Paul addresses believers as "loved by God, called as saints," indicating their holy status through faith. Also, in Philippians 1 6 and 1 Thessalonians 5:23–24, Paul implies a process toward holiness for every believer.

glance, or a family member navigating doubts or pushback from others, hold fast to Matthew 5:10. Your faith steps, though imperfect, shape a home where God's Kingdom shines.

A Guiding Vision

The "Kingdom of Heaven," synonymous with the "Kingdom of God," is God's sovereign rule, manifest both now and in the future. Presently, it is experienced through faith in Jesus, as he declared, "Repent, because the kingdom of heaven has come near" (Matthew 4:17). Jesus' parables, like that of the mustard seed (Matthew 13:31–32), illustrate the Kingdom's growth from small beginnings to transformative impact. In the future, it will be fully realized when Christ returns, as Revelation 11:15 proclaims: "The kingdom of the world has become the kingdom of our Lord and of his Christ." Phillip Yancey, in *The Jesus I Never Knew*, writes,

> The kingdom of heaven, he said elsewhere, is like a treasure of such value that any shrewd investor would "in his joy" sell all he has in order to buy it. It represents value far more real and permanent than anything the world has to offer, for this treasure will pay dividends both here on earth and also in the life to come. Jesus places emphasis not on what we give up but on what we receive.[8]

The Kingdom of Heaven is our guiding vision. By fostering homes where love, mercy, and truth prevail, our family can reflect God's rule. This might mean prioritizing grace in conflicts or teaching family members to value God's will, as prayed in Matthew 6:10: "Your kingdom come. Your will be done." Our home can become a microcosm of God's Kingdom, where his presence and the Scriptures, as the standard of truth, nurture faith and unity. The promise that "the kingdom of heaven is theirs" assures everyone that our efforts, though challenging, are eternally significant. We can excel in problem-solving, co-parenting, and relationship-building, but our efforts aren't the measure of our success in the Kingdom of God; our faithfulness is.

As you parent children who have their own journey to walk with Jesus, remember that you do not have the power to bring about transformation in their hearts. As Paul David Trip reminds us in his book *Parenting*, we cannot force our children's faith, and "we cannot make your children love, believe, surrender, respect, confess, forgive, serve, speak the truth, be pure of heart, and worship God."[9] But you can point them to the One who can.

Discipleship and Our Children

As parents of blended families, we must first put *ourselves* at the feet of Jesus, maintaining a dependent posture and allowing the Holy Spirit to shape us into His likeness so that we can lead our children in the way of Christ. As saints in progress, we're being transformed "from glory to glory" (2 Corinthians 3:18)—a promise that God is shaping us and our children into Christ's image. This gradual journey fuels our discipleship, even when progress feels slow.

In our *Smoothie* family, we have members who are faithfully walking with Jesus, some who are lukewarm in their faith, and others who are not yet believers. Extended family members include atheists, agnostics, and adherents to other faiths. This variety of faith perspectives has become a fertile ground for Jim and me—if not all of us—to grow in our knowledge of the Christian faith, patience in prayer, and dependence on God to move by his power rather than imposing our will upon others.

When our eyes are fixed on Jesus, he can make us into a Christlike wife, husband, stepparent, or co-parent. We must model faith consistently, as Paul writes: "Imitate me, as I also imitate Christ" (1 Corinthians 11:1). This involves being transparent in our growth journey while showing love and grace, especially when children resist. If you're a child or in-law, your honesty about doubts or struggles is part of this journey, too—Jesus invites you to follow him at your own pace. Discipleship is patiently and gently guiding every individual toward Christ.

Each of us has a front-row seat to watch the Lord as he transforms our family members into his disciples. What a privilege! It takes hard work, wisdom, and time to meaningfully guide your family on their journey of faith, even when it hurts. It will require patience and creativity to picture a future filled with flourishing, hope, and God's best. By living out these principles and remaining faithful to our commitment to seek God's best, we can show that faith can thrive in complexity. As Michael J. Wilkins writes in *Following the Master*, "We will go places others have not gone."[10] As saints in progress, embrace your calling to disciple your family, trusting that your faith steps, even through opposition, will bear eternal fruit.

Parenting and discipleship in a blended family are profound callings, rich with opportunities to reflect Jesus' redemptive love and unite in his suffering (Philippians 3:7–10). Even if the journey is marked by opposition and suffering, or perhaps because of it, our family, with all its complexities, can be a powerful witness to God's redemptive grace.

PRACTICAL TOOLS:

- **Self-Reflection Exercise:** Set aside time in a quiet space to reflect on and pray about your role as a disciple of Jesus and a member of your family. Think of a recent moment when you faced opposition or skepticism from within the family about your faith. Write about how it felt and what it revealed about your trust in God. Choose a small, specific action to take this week that reflects faithfulness in the face of this challenge. For parents, align with your spouse on core biblical values; for children, consider how you can show respect and openness to faith discussions.

- **Healing Discussion:** In an informal setting, such as at the dinner table, create space for open talks about faith, struggles, and doubts, fostering growth while staying consistent. Encourage everyone, including children, to share one question or feeling about faith to build understanding.

- **Prayer Prompt:** Ask God for patience and discernment as you share your faith with family members across different backgrounds. Pray for family unity and for strength to respond to "softball" persecutions, like skepticism or resistance, with grace. Pray also for humility to avoid judging others' faith journeys.

- **Beatitudes Reflection:** Reflect on Matthew 5:10–12 in your parenting journey and consider how you have faced challenges in raising your family to follow Jesus and rejoice in signs of spiritual growth, encouraging continued progress.

CHAPTER 9

IDENTITY

AN ENDURING, SHINING LEGACY

You are the salt of the earth. But if the salt should lose its taste,
how can it be made salty?.... You are the light of the world....
Let your light shine before others, so that they may see your
good works and give glory to your Father in heaven.

—MATTHEW 5:13–16

Every other year, our *Smoothie* family gathers for what we affection-ately call a "Smoothie Slam" vacation. As our family grows, finding a home big enough is a challenge, yet our children insist that we pile in together. Picture a house alive with the sounds of children play-ing hide-and-seek or chasing each other with Nerf guns, the clatter of adults planning outings, and the never-ending debate over whether we've bought enough food. The women head out to shop, filling carts at the supermarket and Costco, only to puzzle over where to store it all and how to convince Jim that we'll eat it all by the end of our vacation. Children and in-laws from different households blend together, cre-ating a vibrant, chaotic family experience. We share daily adventures, games, and stories under the stars, even as we navigate the inevitable spills and squabbles.

If this sounds too good to be true, I get it. I am just as surprised as you might be. Years ago, this gathering felt like an impossible dream. Our family was a patchwork of past hurts, clashing traditions, and tentative steps toward unity. Divorce had left scars, and blending our family seemed like trying to merge two different worlds. We were encouraged by a dear friend to create memorable experiences, such as trips and day excursions that build new memories. Inspired by her advice, we started this tradition, and as we leaned on Christ, something miraculous happened: our patchwork family began to reflect God's love, not our brokenness.

Over the years, Jim and I have observed our adult children and their families spend hours chatting, laughing, and enjoying one another. We've seen them care for, support, and challenge each other. They've shared stories from their childhood and dreams for the future. More importantly, we've seen them hold hands as we pray before meals, their voices expressing gratitude to God. They even gather without us—proof that Jesus, not us, holds our family together. These moments bring us profound joy, a glimpse of redemption—a legacy taking root. This transformation didn't happen overnight nor by our power. Yes, it required intentional choices, countless prayers, and a commitment to placing Jesus at the center of our family. Jesus did the heavy lifting of transforming hearts.

A blended family is more than two merged households; it's an opportunity to build a culture that reflects Christ when we trust Him. In this final chapter, we'll explore how Christ calls us to shine as salt and light, and invites us to join in his redemptive work.

Transformed by Faith

Faith in Jesus transforms hearts, reorienting us from self-reliance to dependence on God. The Bible declares, "If anyone is in Christ, he is a new creation; the old has passed away, and see, the new has come!" (2 Corinthians 5:17). This change is profound, and it's caused by the Holy Spirit aligning the hearts of believers with God's will. Let us consider a few short New Testament stories that mirror the hope for blended families—stories that show how Christ can transform both individuals and households.

Zacchaeus, a tax collector despised for his greed, was wealthy but spiritually empty until he encountered Jesus.* Luke writes that Zacchaeus was too short to see through the crowd, so he climbed a tree in faith to glimpse the Savior. Jesus "looked up" to Zacchaeus, called him by name, and dined at his home. Zacchaeus responded with repentance, pledging to give half of his wealth to the poor and repay those he cheated fourfold. His faith in Jesus transformed him from selfishness to generosity. Likewise, as blended families or families dealing with conflict, we often climb uphill to find connection—but Jesus sees, calls, and transforms even the most broken hearts.

The love of Jesus has the power to change not only individual lives but also entire families.

Jairus, a synagogue leader, faced heartbreak when his daughter died. In faith, he humbly sought Jesus. Undeterred by the crowd's doubt, Jesus entered the home, took the girl's hand, and said, "Little girl, I say to you, get up" (Mark 5:41). She rose, and the family's grief turned to joy.† Their faith, deepened by Christ's compassion, was a testimony to the community. Like Jairus' household, we find restoration for our families through trust in Christ. Some dead things (dreams, hopes, traditions) will be brought to life. Some relationships will be reconciled. Jesus, as the Son of God, can intervene in human affairs in extraordinary ways, not only through his divine power, but also through the quiet transformation of our hearts and family as we follow him in faith.

---

* Luke 19:1–10.
† See Mark 5:22–24, 35–42.

Similarly, a royal official in Cana begged Jesus to heal his dying son (John 4:46–53). He traveled far to find Jesus, then pleaded with Jesus to come. But Jesus, moved by the official's faith, sent the scared father home with a promise, "Go...your son will live" (John 4:50). The official trusted those words, and before he reached home, his servants brought good news: his son was alive and healed from his fever. It happened the very moment Jesus commanded the words. "So he himself believed, along with his whole household" (John 4:53). This family's transformation echoes ours, for we trusted in Jesus' promises long before anything changed—and we're trusting him still for miracles only he can achieve.

These stories show how Jesus' intervention not only restores individuals but unites families in faith, turning their homes into places of worship and love.

Like Zacchaeus, Jairus, and the official, blended families—once broken—find restoration through faith in Jesus. By choosing Jesus' ways of grace, love, forgiveness, and discipleship, strained relationships can heal, and love grows. While challenges may still arise from time to time, a strong biblical foundation provides the fertile ground for unity and health to thrive.

The Identity of the Redeemed

As we saw above, an encounter with Jesus can transform us. It's worth thinking about what happens next. What do people who have been changed by Jesus look like? For this point, we turn to the next section of the Sermon on the Mount. These verses form a bridge between the Beatitudes and the rest of the Sermon, shifting from "Blessed are..." to "You are..." statements. While remaining consistent with Jesus' vision for the Kingdom way of being for his disciples, Matthew 5:13-16 issues a call to action.[1] Jesus calls us to be "salt" and "light," not just as individuals but as families. Even a brief study of this section of the Sermon on the Mount will encourage us as families to embrace our role in the Kingdom of God. These words invite your family to radiate God's love, especially amid blending challenges:

> You are the salt of the earth. But if the salt should lose its taste, how can it be made salty? It's no longer good for anything but to be thrown out and trampled under people's feet. You are the light of the world. A city situated on a hill cannot be hidden. No one lights a lamp and puts it under a basket, but rather on a lampstand, and it gives light for all who are in the house. In the same way, let your light shine before others, so that they may see your good works and give glory to your Father in heaven. (Matthew 5:13–16)

Bible teacher Tim Mackie suggests that we consider the imagery of this passage in reverse order, first light and then salt, to evaluate why these two elements form a clear picture of our identity in Christ.[2] In Isaiah, light symbolizes God's wise instruction, which Israel struggled to follow.[*] In Hebrew, the word for light or daylight (ôr) refers not only to something like a lamp or luminary, but also to elements that brighten such as instruction, knowledge, insight, or a spark of inspiration. Think about how a light bulb is used not just to represent the physical object that gives a lamp light, but also a moment of clarity or wisdom. Jesus, the true light, empowers us to live out God's wisdom, illuminating our homes and communities.

In the Bible, Jesus is the "true light that gives light" (John 1:9). This echoes Genesis 1:3, where God speaks light into being, and the prophets who call him its source (Isaiah 45:7; Jeremiah 31:35). Jesus alone has the authority to grant his followers, those who trust in him, the identity and

---

[*] See for example: Isaiah 2:5; 42:6, 16; 50:10.

ability to be light—people who live or walk in God's instruction. As his followers, we embody God's instruction to bring healing, justice, and restoration to this world. So, when he says we are "the light," he calls us to shine by living his wisdom.

Salt, the most widely used condiment in the world, serves as both a preservative and a seasoning. Before refrigeration, salt literally saved lives by keeping foods from rotting. In the Old Testament, God's enduring promises are called a "covenant of salt."* Salt represents the unending nature of God's promises, preserving life and faith.

Okay, just one more thought on this imagery. Jonathan Pennington teaches the Sermon as calling us to reorient our values and habits toward a life that reflects God's desires—not to earn salvation (for it is only by grace that we are saved), but to proclaim it.† "The main point to be made here is that the whole of 5:3-15 can be summed up with 5:16 as an exhortation to a way of being in the world that is visible."[3] When Jesus says, "You are the salt...you are the light," he's not offering a feel-good metaphor. He's proclaiming your identity in him and inviting you and your family to spread flourishing through your witness and good deeds (peacemaking, justice, mercy, love, reconciliation, etc.).[4] Like Moses's radiant face after speaking with the Lord, your family shines when rooted in Christ's wisdom.‡

Preserving and Flourishing

A family centered on Jesus brings flavor, preservation, and transformation to the world around them. A strong, faith-filled family culture isn't dictated by past struggles but is shaped by daily choices of love, forgiveness, and intentional discipleship. Traditions, shared values, and acts of service

---

* Leviticus 2:13; Numbers 18:19; 2 Chronicles 13:5.
† Romans 3:24; 5:2, 15–17; 11:6.
‡ Exodus 34:29.

all play a role in reinforcing biblical principles and strengthening family unity, but Christ must be central. By pursuing a God-centered home, we not only experience healing and connection, but we also serve as a testimony of hope and redemption to others. What was once fractured can be restored; what seemed beyond repair can become a reflection of his grace.

"You are the light of the world...let your light shine before others"—this is the calling for your family in Christ. God redeems not only individuals. He redeems entire households, and he uses imperfect families to showcase his perfect love.* Your family becomes more than a place of healing; it gives birth to a legacy of redemption, blessing generations to come. You are blessed to bless others.

What If Your Family's Story Could Shine?

During a recent Smoothie Slam vacation, some family members engaged in a tough conversation that escalated into an argument that wounded hearts. Hurtful words were exchanged, emotions were bruised, and our family unity was tested. The night dragged on and the next day felt heavy, but the years, prayers, and effort we had invested in creating a Christ-centered family carried us through. Before I left my bedroom that morning, I prayed for all of us; and it turned out others had done the same. The individuals involved in the conflict privately apologized to each other and to those affected. Although it was awkward, everyone did their best to express their emotions respectfully and kindly, agreeing that more conversations would be needed to resolve the underlying issues. I was so relieved they chose forgiveness rather than retaliating or holding grudges.

---

* For examples of families and households redeemed by God through faith, see: Genesis 6:9-8:19 (Noah); Genesis 17:7-27, 18:19 (Abraham); Joshua 2:1-21; 6:17-25 (Rahab); Acts 10:1-48 (Cornelius); Acts 16:25-34 (Philippian Jailer).

The atmosphere in the house that morning started thick with tension, but as the day went on, everyone's mood gradually improved. That argument was an unpleasant experience for all of us, resulting in sadness over the realization that some deep resentments still lingered. However, we had come a long way, for we could talk about it and remain committed to working toward a resolution. After we returned from the trip, those involved met to process and discuss some more, and, thankfully, were able to move forward in unity. There are likely some conversations that still need to be had, but we are more open to them. Every time our family gets together, we are aware of our imperfections, but we're so grateful for how far we've come with the help of Jesus. You'll stumble—tempers will flare, and unity may falter—but no family is beyond God's reach and transformative power.

My family's journey shows how God's grace shines through our imperfections. Here's one more story, included here because many have urged me to share it in this book. From the start of our marriage, Jim and I knew that celebrating the holidays together with our *Smoohie* would be complex, given the many ex-spouses and in-laws involved in our children's lives. They now had to divide their time, visiting multiple households during each holiday. To accommodate this, we hold Thanksgiving and Christmas on different days, usually one or two days later. Though this choice felt necessary at first, I now see it as a blessing. When we gather, everyone arrives relaxed, free from the stress of juggling multiple events in a single day. Our Christmas celebration embraces extended family, friends, and new guests, and we make it a priority to invite those who might feel alone or adrift during the holidays, ensuring they share in the warmth of our blended family. My mother always said, "There is an open seat at our table for a guest." In a way, our families, by their nature, learn to make room for others. Once you're blending, why not add a few more ingredients?

This legacy of making room for others continues in our family today. My son-in-law has committed to adopting my daughter's daughters—my granddaughters—fully embracing them as his own. Similarly, my step-daughter has adopted her stepdaughter, weaving yet another thread of inclusion into our tapestry. Through these acts, God is building an enduring legacy of openness and redemption, showing how he expands our hearts to welcome more.

A cherished tradition at our Christmas gathering is reading a version of the Christmas story I crafted years ago, weaving passages from Genesis to Revelation. Each person reads a sentence or two, and every year, we're reminded of what unites us at our core: Jesus Christ, Immanuel, "God with us."*

As God takes your messy experiences and broken pieces to form a mosaic of grace, your family's story can testify to his love. But it requires daily choices. Will you forgive when it's hard? Will you model grace when tempers flare? Will you make room for others? Will you, like Joshua, choose today to serve the Lord?

> But if it doesn't please you to worship the Lord, choose for yourselves today: Which will you worship...? As for me and my family, we will worship the Lord. (Joshua 24:15)

God can use your family for his glory. Throughout Scripture, God works through imperfect families—Abraham's complex family, Joseph's blended household in Egypt, and even Jesus' own earthly family, the church. Blended families are a powerful testimony of God's grace and ability to bring unity where division once existed.

Here's my challenge (and not really mine, but the Lord Jesus'): Be "salt" and "light" to your home, your neighborhood, and beyond. Teach your

---

* Matthew 1:23.

children to pray, share your love for God and his Word, model forgiveness, and prioritize faith in Jesus. Let your family story reflect the Light that never goes out through acts of service and sharing your testimony. Live so others at least consider or perhaps say, "Their God is real." Imagine your family years from now, children holding the faith you've modeled, grandchildren hearing stories of God's redemption, and a community touched by your love. This is the legacy of redemption—not just healing and unity for today but flourishing for generations.

Picture in your mind a tree planted by a river, its roots firmly fixed on solid ground, but reaching the source of abundant water for nourishment. All around may be a desolate desert with harsh winds and the hot brightness of the sun beating down, but the tree is flourishing and bearing fruit. Such is the image the prophet Jeremiah presents of those who trust in the Lord. It has become our *Smoothie* vision:

> The person who trusts in the Lord, whose confidence indeed is the Lord, is blessed. He will be like a tree planted by water: it sends its roots out toward a stream, it doesn't fear when heat comes, and its foliage remains green. It will not worry in a year of drought or cease producing fruit. (Jeremiah 17:7–8)

As we conclude this book, I'll once again reiterate my conviction: all families can reflect God's redemption, but healthy and united blended families can spotlight it. Israel struggled with obedience, and the disciples struggled at times to be the salt and light. We might too, but remember, Jesus promises, "I am with you always, to the end of the age."* I don't know what challenges we will encounter in the future, but I have hope and a strategy to keep trying. The Beatitudes help me remember that conflict doesn't end our story. One hurtful moment can wound, as I've seen in

---

* Matthew 28:20.

my family and others I pastor; but to the extent that those "left standing" continue to fight for unity in Christ Jesus, our families can continue to flourish. So can yours. Day by day, hour by hour, minute by minute, we are in God's good and loving hands.

I close with the priestly prayer, the one given to Moses by the Lord to bless the Israelites. May it be a blessing for your very own *Smoothie* family:

> May the Lord bless you and protect you; may the Lord make his face shine on you and be gracious to you; may the Lord look with favor on you and give you peace. (Numbers 6:24–26)

May your home overflow with Christ's peace, your love reflect his grace, and your family shine as a beacon of redemption. Amen.

PRACTICAL TOOLS:

- **Self-Reflection Exercise:** What is God prompting you to hold as a vision for your family's spiritual future? Select a family Bible verse reflecting your family's faith values, purpose, and goals. Include your children in the selection process and display the verse prominently in your home. Read it often to remind yourselves of God's faithfulness.

- **Healing Discussion:** Discuss the traditions your family values, collectively and individually. What traditions should be honored? What new traditions can be created together? While there might be areas of brokenness that still need healing, recognize how far your family has come, and encourage one another to keep pursuing God's best.

- **Prayer Prompt:** Pray for Christ to be the foundation of your home and give you wisdom in leading your family in faith. Ask God to use your family as a testimony of his grace and love. Pray for future generations that they will walk in faith.

- **Beatitudes Reflection:** Reflect on Matthew 5:13–16. Consider the way your family is "salt" to one another, how you encourage one another, and where your family has lost its "saltiness" but can be redeemed with the help of Jesus. Also consider how your family currently reflects Christ's light and what areas still need God's healing.

ACKNOWLEDGMENTS

This book is dedicated to our *Smoothie* family, but here is where I want to express my deepest gratitude to them and so many others who have shaped this journey. To my beloved husband, Jim—my "number one fan!" as you like to say—thank you for your unwavering love and support, walking beside me in life and lifting me through this book's creation. To our children, in-laws, and grandchildren, thank you for teaching, challenging, and encouraging Jim and me as we strive to lead with godly wisdom and daily dependence on Jesus. Your love and presence are a blessing, and we pray the Lord's favor upon you.

I'm profoundly grateful for our church community, dear friends, and the life groups my husband Jim and I have had the privilege of joining over the years. Though I can't name everyone, if you're reading this, know that your prayers have carried us through trials and deepened our trust in Jesus. Your safe, accountable spaces have been a cornerstone of our growth. Special thanks to the blended and non-blended families who've modeled Christlike grace and to the men in Jim's long-standing men's group, whose enduring marriages inspire us. You remind us that every family can uplift others.

To Jim Burns, who penned the foreword, thank you for your wisdom, kindness, and expertise in family and marriage. Your endorsement and introduction mean the world. I'm also grateful for leaders like Senior Pastor Eric Geiger, Pastor Emeritus Kenton Beshore, and Dr. John Townsend, whose anointed teaching has anchored us in God's truth. A special note of thanks to Pastor Eric Heard of Mariners Church, our cherished *Smoothie* family pastor, who has officiated most of our family's weddings, counseled us through crises, and always offered wisdom and support with an open heart.

My heartfelt thanks go to the experts who reviewed this manuscript: Dr. Jonathan T. Pennington, Dr. John Townsend, Ron L. Deal, Dr. Jenna Flowers, Dr. Eric Geiger, and Dr. Ed Stetzer. Your insights and editorial feedback sharpened this work. To our early readers cohort, your enthusiasm and thoughtful reflections helped shape this book—thank you!

To my publishing team, I owe immense gratitude. First, to my daughter, Kayleigh Antenucci, Trochia Ministry Director, your tireless efforts and encouragement kept me on track, helping me complete this manuscript in record time. I love you dearly! To Jessica Snell, your developmental edits transformed this book into something I believe will bless many—thank you for your outstanding partnership. To the team at Fedd Books, your commitment to excellence and storytelling has made this process a joy. To my editor, Nydia Stecky, for your invaluable guidance and kind encouragement. I am so glad the content of the book ministered to you personally and led you to challenge me to share this message with all families, not just blended ones. Thank you for refining this work with care and making it accessible to all, even though it is still written with blended families in mind.

From the bottom of my heart, thank you all for making this book possible. To God be the glory!

ENDNOTES

INTRODUCTION

1   Jack O. Balswick, Judith K. Balswick, and Thomas V. Frederick, *The Family: A Christian Perspective on the Contemporary Home* (Grand Rapids, MI: BakerAcademic, 2021), 303.

2   Kasey J. Eickmeyer, *American Children's Family Structure: Two Biological Parent Families*, Bowling Green State University, https://www.bgsu.edu/ncfmr/resources/data/family-profiles/eickmeyer-two-biological-parent-families-fp-17-15.html accessed on July 15, 2025.

3   Kristin McCarthy, M.Ed., "Blended Family Statistics: A Deeper Look Into the Structure," Love to Know, updated August 5, 2021, https://www.lovetoknow.com/parenting/parenthood/blended-family-statistics.

4   C. S. Lewis, *God in the Dock* (Grand Rapids: William B. Eerdmans, Co., 1970), pp. 284–286.

5   "Reflections: Creating Christian Family," the C. S. Lewis Institute, accessed online on March 20, 2025, https://www.cslewisinstitute.org/resources/reflections-june-2007/.

6   Servais Pinckaers, *The Pursuit of Happiness—God's Way: Living the Beatitudes*, trans. Mary Thomas Noble (Eugene, OR: Wipf & Stock, 1998), 36–37.

7   Jonathan T. Pennington, *The Sermon on the Mount and Human Flourishing: A Theological Commentary* (Grand Rapids, MI: Baker Academic, 2017), 64.

8   Pennington, *The Sermon on the Mount and Human Flourishing*, 51.

9   Pennington, *The Sermon on the Mount and Human Flourishing*, 54.

10 Pennington, *The Sermon on the Mount and Human Flourishing*, 54, 144.

11 Balswick, Balswick, and Frederick, *The Family*, 277.

12 Jerry Bridges, *Trusting God* (Colorado Springs, CO: NavPress, 2008), 199.

CHAPTER 1

1   Leo Tolstoy, *Anna Karenina*, translated by Constance Garnett (New York, NY: Modern Library, 2000), 1.

2   "Anna Karenina principle," Wikipedia, accessed on March 14, 2025, https://en.wikipedia.org/wiki/Anna_Karenina_principle.

3   Gabor Maté, with Daniel Maté, *The Myth of Normal: Illness, Health, and Healing in a Toxic Culture* (UK: Penguin Random House, 2022), 7.

4   APA Dictionary of Psychology: dysfunctional family, accessed online July 1, 2025, https://dictionary.apa.org/dysfunctional-family/.

5   "The Dysfunctional Family," the Institute of Counseling in Nigeria, accessed online March 20, 2025, https://instituteofcounseling.org/the-dysfunctional-family/.

6   Jane Hunt, *Dysfunctional Family: Making Peace with Your Past* (Carol Stream, ILL: Aspire Press, 2014).

7   David E. Garland and Diana R. Garland, *Flawed Families of the Bible: How God's Grace Works through Imperfect Relationships* (Grand Rapids, MI: Brazos Press, 2007), 13.

8   Garland and Garland, *Flawed Families of the Bible*, p. 14.

9   Pennington, *The Sermon on the Mount and Human Flourishing*, 153.

10   Pennington, *The Sermon on the Mount and Human Flourishing*, 154.

CHAPTER 2

1   Evan Owens and Jenny Owens, *Healing What's Hidden: Practical Steps to Overcoming Trauma* (Grand Rapids: MI, Revell, 2022), 25.

2   Mark Wolynn, *It Didn't Start with You: How Inherited Family Trauma Shapes Who We Are and How to End the Cycle* (New York: NY, Penguin Books, 2017), 1.

3   Maté and Maté, *The Myth of Normal*, 20.

4   Maté and Maté, *The Myth of Normal*, 20–21.

5   Maté and Maté, *The Myth of Normal*, 22.

6   Maté and Maté, *The Myth of Normal*, 23.

7   See Adrian Bird's 2007 article *"Perceptions of epigenetics,"* Nature, 447(7143), 396–398, https://doi.org/10.1038/nature05913, accessed March 26, 2025.

8   Wolynn, *It Didn't Start with You*.

9   Wolynn, *It Didn't Start with You*, 15.

10   John W. James and Russell Friedman, *The Grief Recovery Handbook: The Action Program for Moving Beyond Death, Divorce. and Other Losses* (New York: NY, HarperCollins Publishers, 1998), 5.

11   Pinckaers, *The Pursuit of Happiness*, 77.

12   Mariel Buqué, Ph.D., *Break the Cycle: A Guide to Healing Intergenerational Trauma* (New York, Penguin Random House, 2024), 4.

13   Harriet Lerner, *Why Don't You Apologize? Healing Big Betrayals and Everyday Hurts* (New York: NY, Touchstone, 2017), 141.

CHAPTER 3

1   Ron L. Deal, *The Smart Stepfamily: 7 Steps to a Healthy Family* (Bloomington, MN: Bethany House Publishers, 2014), 207.

2   Peter Wohlleben, *The Hidden Life of Trees: What They Feel, How They Communicate—Discoveries from a Secret World*, trans. Jane Billinghurst (Vancouver: Greystone Books, 2016).

3   Genesis 1:26–31.

4   Murray Bowen, *Family Therapy in Clinical Practice* (New York: Jason Aronson, 1978).

5   Michael E. Kerr, *Bowen Theory's Secrets: Revealing the Hidden Life of Families* (New York: NY, 2019), 31.

6   Albert Bandura, *Social Learning Theory* (Englewood Cliffs, NJ: Prentice Hall, 1977).

7   http://www.apa.org/, accessed April 3, 2025.

8   Patricia L. Papernow, *Surviving and Thriving in Stepfamily Relationships: What Works and What Doesn't* (New York: Routledge, 2013).

9   Salvador Minuchin, *Families and Family Therapy* (Cambridge, MA: Harvard University Press, 1974).

10   Dr. Henry Cloud and Dr. John Townsend, *Boundaries: When to Say Yes, How to Say No to Take Control of Your Life* (Grand Rapids, MI: Zondervan Books, 2017) 134.

11   *Journal of Marriage and Family* 2021.

12   Kerr, *Bowen Theory's Secrets*, 31.

13   Andrew Murray, *Humility; The Journey Toward Holiness* (Minneapolis, MN: Bethany House, 2001), 17.

14   Andrew Murray, *Humility*, 57.

15   Pinckaers, *The Pursuit of Happiness*, 61.

16   Chapman, Gary, and Ron L. Deal, *Building Love Together in Blended Families: The 5 Love Languages and Becoming Stepfamily Smart* (Chicago: Northfield Publishing, 2020).

17   Kerr, Michael E., and Murray Bowen, *Family Evaluation: An Approach Based on Bowen Theory*, (New York: W.W. Norton & Company, 1988).

18   Papernow, *Surviving and Thriving in Stepfamily Relationships*.

19   Chapman and Deal, *Building Love Together in Blended Families*.

20   Chapman and Deal, *Building Love Together in Blended Families*.

21   Pinckaers, *The Pursuit of Happiness*, 72.

CHAPTER 4

1   Ed Stetzer, *Marriage, Divorce and the Church: What Do the Stats Say, and Can Marriage Be Happy?* Accessed April 11, 2025, https://churchleaders.com/pastors/pastor-articles/297689-marriage-divorce-church-stats-say-can-marriage-happy.html.

2   Shaunti Feldhahn and Tally Whitehead, *The Good News About Marriage: Debunking Discouraging Myths about Marriage and Divorce* (Sister, OR: Multnomah, 2014).

3   Andy Crouch, *The Tech-Wise Family: Everyday Steps for Putting Technology in Its Proper Place* (Grand Rapids, MI: Baker Books, 2017), 34.

4   Timothy Keller, *The Meaning of Marriage: Facing the Complexities of Commitment with the Wisdom of God* (New York, NY: Penguin Random House, 2011), 87.

5   Deal, *The Smart Stepfamily*, 53.

6   Ron L. Deal & David H. Olson, *The Smart Stepfamily Marriage: Keys to Success in the Blended Family* (Bloomington, MN: Bethany House, 2015), 112.

7   Deal, *The Smart Stepfamily*, 27.

8   Michael Card, *Inexpressible: Hesed and the Mystery of God's Lovingkindness* (Downers Grove, IL: InterVarsity Press, 2018), 41.

9   Saint Athanasius, trans. J. Behr (original work published ca. 318 CE), *On the Incarnation* (Yonkers, NY: St. Vladimir's Seminary Press), 56.

10   Dietrich Bonhoeffer, *Life Together* (New York, NY: Harper One, 1954), 30.

11   Philip Yancey, *The Jesus I Never Knew* (Grand Rapids, MI: Zondervan, 1999), 159.

12   Pinckaers, *The Pursuit of Happiness*, 107.

CHAPTER 5

1   Ike Miller, *Good Baggage: How Your Difficult Childhood Prepared You for Healthy Relationships* (Grand Rapids, MI: Baker Books, 2023).

2   John Bradshaw, *Homecoming: Reclaiming and Healing Your Inner Child* (New York, NY: Bantaan Book, 1992).

3   Pinckaers, *The Pursuit of Happiness*, 117.

4   Owens and Owens, *Healing What's Hidden*.

CHAPTER 6

1   "Mental Health," *APA Dictionary of Psychology*, American Psychological Association, *accessed May 5, 2025*, https://dictionary.apa.org/mental-health.

2   Peter Scazzero, *Emotionally Healthy Spirituality: It's Impossible to Be Spiritually Mature, While Remaining Emotionally Immature* (Grand Rapids, MI: Zondervan, 2017), 211.

3   Scazzero, *Emotionally Healthy Spirituality*, 23.

4   Visit https://www.emotionallyhealthy.org/you/

5   Brené Brown, *Atlas of the Heart: Mapping Meaningful Connection and the Language of Human Experience* (New York, NY: Random House, 2021), 12.

6   Pinckaers, *The Pursuit of Happiness*, 140.

7   Pinckaers, *The Pursuit of Happiness*, 135.

8   Chris Voss and Tahl Raz, *Never Split the Difference: Negotiating As If Your Life Dependend On It* (New York, NY: Harper Business, 2016), 15.

9   Scazzero, *Emotionally Healthy Spirituality*, 145.

CHAPTER 7

1   William Arndt et al., *A Greek-English Lexicon of the New Testament and Other Early Christian Literature* (Chicago: University of Chicago Press, 2000), 288.

2   Dr. James H. Bray and John Kelly, *Step Families: Love, Marriage, and Parenting in the First Decade* (New York, NY: Broadway Books, 1998).

3   Pinckaers, *The Pursuit of Happiness*, 146.

4   John Boardman, et al. *The Oxford History of the Classical World* (New York, NY: Oxford University Press, 1986) 208–210.

5   Voss and Raz, *Never Split the Difference*, 26.

6   Erich Fromm, *The Art of Loving* (New York, NY: HarperCollins, 1956), 4.

7   Jenna Flowers, PsyD, LMFT, *The Conscious Parent's Guide to Coparenting* (Avon, MA: Adams Media, 2016), 15.

8   Paul David Tripp, *Parenting: 14 Gospel Principles That Can Radically Change Your Family* (Wheaton, IL: Crossway, 2024), 33.

9   Pinckaers, *The Pursuit of Happiness*, 156.

CHAPTER 8

1   Pennington, *The Sermon on the Mount and Human Flourishing*, 117.

2   Dietrich Bonhoeffer, *Works*, volume 4, *Discipleship*, trans. Martin Kuske and Ilse Tōdt (Minneapolis, MN: Fortress Press, 2003), 87.

3   Arndt et al., *A Greek-English Lexicon of the New Testament and Other Early Christian Literature*, 254.

4   Pinckaers, *The Pursuit of Happiness*, 172.

5   J. Ramsey Michaels, *1 Peter*, vol. 49, Word Biblical Commentary (Dallas: Word, Incorporated, 1988), 29.

6   Bonhoeffer, *Discipleship*, 87.

7   Larry Chouinard, *Matthew*, The College Press NIV Commentary (Joplin, MO: College Press, 1997), Mt. 5:11–12.

8   Philip Yancey, *The Jesus I Never Knew*, 125.

9   Paul David Tripp, *Parenting*, 192.

10   Michael J. Wilkins, *Following the Master: A Biblical Theology of Discipleship* (Grand Rapids, MI: Zondervan, 1992) 348.

CHAPTER 9

1   Pennington, *The Sermon on the Mount and Human Flourishing*, 119.

2   To listen to the Bible Project podcast on Salt and Light, visit https://bibleproject.com/podcast/salt-land-and-light-world/, accessed May 30, 2025.

3   Pennington, *The Sermon on the Mount and Human Flourishing*, 167.

4   Pennington, *The Sermon on the Mount and Human Flourishing*, 119.

ALSO AVAILABLE FROM INÉS FRANKLIN

Uncharted: Navigating Your Unique Journey of Faith & 8-Week Study Guide

(Online Course and Teaching videos are available at www.trochia.org/courses/uncharted)

In a world full of obstacles, comparison, and uncertainty, the most rewarding journey you will ever undertake is the uncharted walk with God.

- Know God's desires for you
- Learn the key to overcoming any challenge
- Experience blessing through spiritual practices
- Build a faith that lasts

Available at Amazon and trochia.org/store

Inexplorado: Navegando Por Tu Camino Único de Fe

En un mundo lleno de obstáculos, comparación e incertidumbre, el viaje más gratificante que emprenderás jamás es el camino inexplorado con Dios.

- Conoce los deseos de Dios para ti
- Aprende la clave para superar cualquier desafío
- Experimenta la bendición a través de Prácticas Espirituales
- Construye una fe que perdura

Disponible en Amazon y trochia.org/store

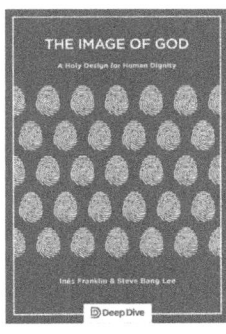

The Image of God – Workbook and Teaching Videos

*An 8-week group-discipleship experience that unveils the beautiful, biblical understanding of human life, dignity, and worth, rooted in God's original and beautiful design for his beloved people. This study is one of three studies from the **Deep Dive Series**.*

*Available at **experiencerooted.com***

For more information:
inesfranklin.com and **trochia.org/store**

Trochia Ministries is a 501(c)3 nonprofit organization whose mission is to meet people where they are and help them know and grow in Christ through practical resources, biblical teaching, and grace-filled mentoring. Hundreds of resources created by Trochia are freely available online and on social media. Trochia also publishes Christian discipleship books, small group studies, and podcasts.

Igniting wholehearted faith in Jesus that transforms lives and generations.

- Embrace Jesus's grace to heal, grow, and live with resilience and integrity.
- Experience how God redeems individuals and families to showcase his love across generations.
- Deepening faith through Scripture, prayer, and rhythms that draw us closer to God.

trochia.org

Social media:

@trochiaministries

@inesfranklin

The Journey We Share Podcast | Faith and Life Uncharted

Join Inés Franklin and her daughter, Kayleigh Antenucci, as they dive deep into the realities of faith, family, and life's unexpected paths. Together, they explore family dynamics, faith journeys across generations, and the challenges and joys of spiritual growth.

YouTube.com/@trochia